Hermeneutic philosophy and the sociology of art

International Library of Sociology

Founded by Karl Mannheim
Editor: John Rex, University of Warwick

Arbor Scientiæ
Arbor Vitæ

A catalogue of the books available in the **International Library of Sociology** and other series of Social Science books published by Routledge & Kegan Paul will be found at the end of this volume.

Hermeneutic philosophy and the sociology of art

An approach to some of the epistemological problems of the sociology of knowledge and the sociology of art and literature

Janet Wolff

Department of Sociology
University of Leeds

Routledge & Kegan Paul

London and Boston

First published in 1975
by Routledge & Kegan Paul Ltd
Broadway House, 68–74 Carter Lane,
London EC4V 5EL and
9 Park Street,
Boston, Mass. 02108, USA
Set in 10 on 11 point Times New Roman
and printed in Great Britain by
Western Printing Services Ltd, Bristol
© *Janet Wolff 1975*

ISBN 0 7100 8048 4

Contents

CONTENTS

Acknowledgments

This book was originally written as a PhD thesis in the Department of Sociology, University of Birmingham. I would like to thank Professor W. Baldamus, Professor Z. Bauman, Stuart Hall, Professor C. Madge, Dr Maurice Roche and Professor P. Winch for their valuable comments, criticisms and encouragement during the writing of the thesis and re-writing of the book; Anna Dwyer for help with the translations from German; Ruth Hemingway, Margaret Knight and Elizabeth McHale for secretarial help; and the Social Science Research Council for financial support while I was still at Birmingham.

I would also like to thank J. C. B. Mohr (Paul Siebeck), Tübingen, for permission to quote (in translation) from their publication, *Wahrheit und Methode*, by H.-G. Gadamer.

Introduction

This book was initially conceived as an examination of the theoretical foundation of the sociology of art and literature. For a number of reasons, many of them recognised and acknowledged by sociologists in the area of the arts, it seemed to me that this study has never been adequately conceived by its practitioners, and in this it has lagged behind even those other branches of the sociology of knowledge—of science, of religion, of ideology—with their still unresolved theoretical issues and debates. This state of under-development is, I believe, to a very large extent due to the nature of the subject-matter in question. In short, I would maintain that the deficiencies involved in any sociological study of art can only be eliminated by a proper attention to the *art* itself. The sociology of art, that is, necessarily includes aesthetics. The constant dilemma of sociologists of art, in the face of the multiplicity of possible levels of analysis and types of data, will only be resolved by the development of a more general theory of art and society, which itself can serve as a guide to the researcher confronted by the twin problems of which aspects of social structure and social life he is to take as significant, and which aspects of the works of art in question—their documentary content, their style, their technical qualities, their art–historical features, or their formal attributes. Thus, I felt that there is at this time a critical need for a sound theoretical foundation for the sociology of art.

However, in the course of my preliminary attempts to formulate the conceptual and methodological questions which seemed to me to be crucial, it became clear that a more general theoretical discussion was necessary, both in the sociology of knowledge and in the methodology and epistemology of the social and cultural sciences, before one could even begin to develop a more specific sociological theory of the arts. This book, then, while maintaining its original intention to show the direction of an adequate sociology of art and

1

literature, in fact remains a study in the sociology of knowledge. I shall suggest that a phenomenological approach has much to recommend it in this context, and that its refinement in hermeneutic philosophy and sociology goes a long way towards the resolution of many of the theoretical problems involved. In discussing and clarifying, if not necessarily always solving, some of the important philosophical issues in this field, the constant underlying reference will be to the creative and artistic-expressive areas of knowledge, in the hope that a better understanding of the social nature and genesis of *all* knowledge may point the way towards a similar comprehension of art and society. Somewhat in the manner of a prologue, therefore, I begin with a brief account of the unsatisfactory state of the sociology of art as it exists at present, together with some preliminary and tentative suggestions as to the methodological foundations which, if adopted, would prove to be an important first step in its improvement. In the following chapters, I shall return to the analysis of knowledge—to the theory of knowledge, the sociology of knowledge, and the methodological problems involved in looking at and understanding knowledge.

My central argument is that hermeneutic philosophy avoids many of the difficulties of the traditional approaches to the sociology of knowledge. In relation to phenomenological sociology, too, the most important aspect of hermeneutics is its structural and historical perspective. I have also tried to show why, within the limits of both positivism and phenomenology, the concept of a world-view, or total ideology—a concept central to the sociology of culture and the sociology of art—remains problematic. The structuralism of both Lévi-Strauss and Goldmann, as well as Durkheim's concept of *conscience collective* and Parsons's 'central value-system', are also unsatisfactory solutions to this particular problem. My suggestion is that Gadamer's hermeneutic philosophy of history (with certain important qualifications and revisions) combines what is best in the structural and phenomenological approaches, and may form the basis of a new and more comprehensive sociology of knowledge and of art.

1 The sociology of art and the sociology of knowledge

The sociology of art and literature is an ill-defined and amorphous discipline, comprising numerous empirical studies and various attempts at rather more general theory, all of which have in common merely the fact that they are somehow concerned with the relationship of art and society. Thus, the sociologist of literature may investigate the social basis of authorship (Laurenson 1969), the sociology of production and distribution of works of literature (Escarpit 1968), literature in primitive society (Radin 1960; Leach 1967), the relationship of values expressed in literature and values of society (Albrecht 1954 and 1956), and historical data relating to literature and society (Goldmann 1964; Altick 1957; Lowenthal 1967; Watt 1967; Webb 1955). Sociologists of art have studied primitive art (Smith 1961; Wingert 1962), art at different historical periods (Antal 1947), the social background of artists (Pelles 1963), the relationship of class and artistic taste (Kavolis 1965), and more general problems of art in society (John Berger 1969; Fischer 1964; Francastel 1951; Hauser 1951; Read 1967). Most of this work consists of empirical studies. On the other hand, attempts have been made to provide a general theory of art in society (Sorokin 1947) or Marxist theories of art (Hauser 1951; Fischer 1964). But what now seems to be needed is a sociology of art at the level of meaning. Such a sociology of art would be equipped to deal with many of the problems in the field which most of the other methods and approaches have to ignore and leave unexplained. One of the most important advantages of the approach I am suggesting is that the *content* of the works of art will be considered as relevant to the question of the sociology of art; the works will not then merely be taken as the data for social science, a procedure which necessarily (although often with some unease) overlooks the question which is surely crucial, namely: what *is* a work of art? The argument here, of course, runs

3

that this question is one of aesthetics, of the philosophy of art, and of the history of art. The reply, in any case, is normative, and involves, in part at least, evaluation of the products. And social science, in so far as it *is* social science, cannot evaluate anything. This is why it has to take as given those objects defined by others as art, and investigate their relationship to other social facts. The trouble is that by accepting uncritically a rather arbitrary definition, sociologists may be overlooking other material, or ignoring distinctions, which could be relevant. Furthermore, others' definitions of what counts as art are far from unanimous, which presents the sociologist with the initial problem of *what* to take as his data. A sociology of art at the level of meaning should be able to talk about the works of art themselves, in discussing their place in social life.

Before I consider the other advantages of a 'Verstehen' sociology, I should like to make clear my position on this well-worn methodological issue. The anti-positivism, anti-behaviouralism which I advocate and defend is more the result of choice than of methodological conviction. I have come to this conclusion during readings and discussions on methodology, when I have found myself resisting the arguments of anti-positivists, and insisting that they have taken their case too far. Verstehende, or phenomenological, sociology is *a* way of doing sociology; it has certain advantages over its alternatives, and (for non-sociological reasons) it is the approach to which I am committed. But positivistic sociology achieves its own results. At its best, it proceeds in a perfectly valid manner, and can often work in areas to which there is little access for Verstehen. Thus, I cannot accept the final step of the argument of those sociologists who, after demonstrating the uniqueness of the phenomenological approach, reject positivism as totally misconceived.[1] (The epistemological naïvety of what Parsons calls 'radical positivism', on the other hand, is clearly not to be endorsed.)[2]

A longer discussion of this particular methodological issue is probably necessary for me to defend the position I have taken, but as it is not essential to the main argument of this chapter, it will have to be omitted here. What *is* required is a brief exposition of the method I am advocating, since there will be reference to 'phenomenological sociology' and the method of Verstehen throughout the following pages. (In a later chapter, I shall consider some of the inadequacies of phenomenological sociology itself, and suggest that these might be supplemented by hermeneutic philosophy and ideology-critique.)

Max Weber (1947b, pp. 80ff) argued that the sociologist must be concerned with the *meaning* of social action—that is, with the

---

[1] See, for example, McHugh's article (1971).
[2] The limitations of naïve positivism will be discussed in chapters 2 and 3.

4

meaning attached to his act by an actor, and by those around him. Action (as opposed to behaviour) is meaningful by definition, and sociology, in so far as it deals with social action, must operate at the level of meaning. Weber's argument is the basis of other, more recent, attacks on positivistic sociology (for example, Jack Douglas's (1967) critique of Durkheim). As a re-definition of the scope and method of social science, the introduction of this new approach has made possible many important works in this particular sociological tradition. It remained for Alfred Schutz to elaborate what Weber had taken for granted: namely the nature and origin of the actor's 'meanings', and the epistemology of the method of Verstehen (Schutz 1972). Verstehen-sociology now appears as phenomenological sociology. (As Schutz maintains, this was implicit in Weber's work, and is not something imposed or added by him.) Sociologists since Schutz (whose book, one of his early works, was first published in 1932) have used the term 'phenomenological' more or less rigorously, but, perhaps with the exception of Schutz himself, who started his academic career as a philosopher, and whose work was approved by Husserl at one stage, I think it would be fair to say that none of the sociologists calling themselves phenomenologists would have been recognised as such by the phenomenologists of pure philosophy. I shall be discussing the method of phenomenology and the phenomenological analysis of the social world later (chapter 2). Here, the point should simply be made that the so-called 'phenomenological method' in the social sciences is by no means the rigorous exercise developed by Husserl and other philosophers. This is not necessarily a criticism, of course. Weber's more primitive notion of Verstehen has proved both methodologically acceptable and extremely useful in practice, without the philosophical justification of a phenomenological foundation. The simple, more intuitive, grasp of meaning and motive is adequate for the study of human action and behaviour (with the usual requirements of scientific method, of objectivity in dealing with even these subjective facts). What such a sociology is *not*, is a comprehensive theory of knowledge (Husserl's 'rigorous science'). It returns to the epistemological status of all the sciences— methodologically sound, but epistemologically as precarious as Descartes's destruction of knowledge originally left them. The sciences, including the social sciences, can and do proceed perfectly well, oblivious of their uncertain foundation.

An essay by Tiryakian (1965) is an attempt to extrapolate from the sociological tradition an existential-phenomenological method. If it is admitted that these terms are imported from philosophy in a somewhat loose way, as I have argued, then it is clearly beside the point to criticise Tiryakian by insisting that one of the writers he mentions is definitely *not* a phenomenologist. I *would* dispute his

5

inclusion of, for example, Parsons, Sorokin and Durkheim, however, for not only are they not phenomenologists, but it is hard to see how they are at all concerned with what Tiryakian calls 'subjective realism'. His uncritical switch from talking about the phenomenological apprehension of individual meanings to that of cultural wholes or social groups is extremely dubious; certainly it requires justification, and cannot simply be presented as unproblematic. (The question of the possibility of grasping supra-individual and inter-subjective facts, such as ideologies, institutions and cultural products, by the phenomenological method, will be discussed below—chapter 4.) However, the significance of the article is that it makes explicit what *is*, in some ways, a common current amongst certain important sociologists. This is interesting historically; it would have been more useful to provide, as well as a historical survey, a description of the existential-phenomenological method in sociology—the ideal to which all these writers are said to approximate.

Rather than examine the differences and convergences of a number of theorists, I propose to define and describe the method first, and then see where the coincidences are with certain sociologists. The approach I envisage for the sociology of knowledge, and, more specifically, the sociology of art and literature, proceeds via the phenomenological understanding of the individual in his social situation, of the patterns of meanings which make up his reality, and of his definition of the situations in which he acts and interacts with others. Schutz, having got this far, thought he had to make the transition from psychology to sociology by introducing the notion of *inter*-subjectivity—a kind of joint experiencing, more or less immediate and direct, by two or more people. Although it remains the case (as he himself acknowledges) that there is inevitably a jump from the pure consciousness which alone can be investigated by phenomenology, to the experience of the other, his analysis is extremely lucid and enlightening. (Perhaps, indeed, by pointing out this one limitation, he has shown once and for all that sociology can never be phenomenologically pure.) However, as Berger and Luckmann's (1967) work makes clear, even without this epistemological justification, phenomenological psychology is already part of sociology; those who accept the tenet of the sociology of knowledge will not deny that the very consciousness which the philosopher or psychologist looks at is social in origin and in content. The world of the individual is formed in and out of an essentially social context.

Thus it is clear that there are two kinds of problem in the application of phenomenology to society. The first, dealt with by Schutz, concerns the fundamental validity of *inter*-personal understanding; in this case, of the sociologist understanding his subject. The second, taking for granted this possibility of sociological understanding, concerns the object of this understanding; the question is how one can get beyond the individual social actor, to social groups and cultural products, still within the framework of a phenomenological method. It is the second problem which will concern us at various points in this book. For example, it will have to be discussed in relation to the concept of the Weltanschauung, when this is applied to a whole social group. For the moment, Berger and Luckmann's example suffices to demonstrate the practicability of a phenomenological sociology of knowledge. It is restricted to a specific type of knowledge, namely the individual's knowledge of society itself (i.e. a sociology of social knowledge). I hope it will prove possible to present an analogous programme for the sociology of art.

Berger and Luckmann show how society exists as subjective reality in the individual consciousness, and how it subsequently, through a process of objectification and reification, appears as objective reality. Like society, art is a creation of individual members, who, in their turn, are in many ways formed *by* society. Thus it should be feasible to examine the social content of art. (The question of art as an individual creation, and therefore subject-matter only for psychology, versus art as, in some sense, an *inter*-individual creation, in the way Berger and Luckmann show society to be, and thus the object of sociology, will also be discussed below. The social element in even an individual creation, however, is to be emphasised here.) I am less concerned with the way in which something which was originally a human product takes on the false appearance of an objective fact (social customs, rules, institutions), than with the primary process of its creation. That is, in the context of art and literature, the social origin of works of art must be taken into account, as well as the way in which their content can be said to relate to social life, without considering the question of how works of art, or styles of art, become removed from their source, and impose themselves as eternal, or at least permanent modes of expression. (Clearly such an analysis would deviate in many ways from that of the objectification of social knowledge. The specific acts of creation are much more available for observation, and thus less hypothetical; the products themselves are material objects, and so, again, observable in a way in which institutions are not; and finally, tradition in art is much more easily recognised *as* tradition than in the case of social knowledge, at least in a society where diverse traditions co-exist, and new styles are created.) Like Berger and Luckmann, then, my intention is to describe the origin and creation of cultural products in social life, from the methodological perspective of the social individual, and of the phenomenology of the social world.

Although none of the phenomenologically-orientated sociologists has so far turned to the sociology of the arts, there are a number of hints in some of their writings on the manner in which they would have proceeded. Schutz's essays are most suggestive here. Some of these, indeed, are in fact small-scale studies of art in social life: not a theory of the sociology of art, but a sociology of art in practice. From these, one can extract the elements of the theoretical orientation. (See, for example, 'Making music together: a study in social relationship', and 'Mozart and the philosophers', Schutz 1964.) More important, in the theoretical essays themselves, there is mention of art and its place in society. In the book referred to above (Schutz 1972), Schutz suggests how his method of sociological understanding, via the extension of inter-subjectivity in the direction of more and more indirect experience and ideal typification, can extend also to cultural *products*. These are merely objectivations, in which the other's subjective experiences manifest themselves (op. cit. p. 133). Thus, besides considering their *objective* meaning (i.e. disregarding their production), we should be able to study their *subjective* meaning. As Schutz phrases it, to do so would be 'to run over in our minds, in simultaneity or quasi-simultaneity, the polythetic acts which constituted the experience of the producer' (p. 133).

It is obvious that the closer one is in experience to the producer, the easier this will be. From a cultural context further removed, the possibility of re-creating his polythetic acts is diminished. Furthermore, at this existential distance it becomes clear that considering the man simply as artistic producer is not only inadequate but impossible. It is necessary to re-create also what can be taken for granted in a more immediate context; that is, the person's art can be understood only in the wider situation of his *total* experiential structure. It might be argued that this is by definition the task of the sociologist of art. The fact is, though, that it has in most cases been thought sufficient to relate the two disparate areas of the arts on the one hand, and some other specific factor of social life (class, for example) on the other. I would maintain that this is the reason why most sociology of art to date is unsatisfactory and limited in explanatory power, not only on the level of meaning, but on any level.

As long as we do not abandon the existential-phenomenological level, it will be impossible to forget the intrinsic relevance of all aspects of the actor's world of meaning. In the next chapter, the constitution of this world will be discussed in detail, together with the place of artistic creativity in the existential reality. In anticipation of that discussion, it is perhaps worth raising here the related question of *how* different provinces of meaning co-exist in the individual consciousness, and in a society. Again, it is Schutz who provides the best account ('On multiple realities' and 'Symbol, reality and society', Schutz 1967). He had argued in *The phenomenology of the social world* that the various provinces of meaning must cohere in the overall meaning-structure of the individual's world, and he explains these different provinces of meaning as 'multiple realities'. The difference between the various realities lies in the nature of the epoché (or bracketing) performed. For example, the natural attitude, that of everyday life, suspends doubts about the world; the province of scientific thought, on the other hand, examines these doubts, but suspends subjectivity, the thinker's own bodily existence and pragmatic relevances. We move from one reality to another with a 'leap' or 'shock'. This is a 'radical modification in the tension of our consciousness, founded in a different *attention à la vie*' ('On multiple realities', p. 232). Throughout, however, the paramount reality is that of everyday life ('Symbol, reality and society'). If we carry this type of analysis into the province of artistic creativity, not only will we have a way of explaining it, but we are also half-way towards solving the old problem of the philosophy of art, of what it is to see (hear, etc.) an object (product) *as* art; of what the artistic content is, for example, of a religious painting; of what the relationship of function to aesthetic quality is; and of whether Duchamp was right when he claimed that anything is art if it is put forward as art, and exhibited a bicycle wheel as a work of art. If, as Schutz says, the province of art is defined by the mode of attention applied to the objects, then indeed anything *can* be art. Other phenomenologists of aesthetics appear to concur, in slightly different terms, with Schutz. (See, for example, Bensman and Lilienfeld 1968; Natanson 1962; Dufrenne 1967; Ingarden 1960 and 1961.)

The real problem, however, is to discover the relations between the multiple realities existing or potential in a single consciousness. Schutz demonstrates the possibility of different modes of consciousness and different kinds of intentionality, without reference to the *content* of the various realities. It is my contention that this is the crucial factor, for any analysis of the constitution of consciousness (i.e. not its *a priori* categories, but its empirical, experiential constitution) will show a certain congruence of all its aspects and, in short, a coherent, meaningfully integrated total world. This brings us back again to the realisation that the province of art, whatever kind of phenomenological reality this is, co-exists with other realities, and notably that of the natural attitude of everyday life, and that its content (its beliefs, perceptions, evaluations) is to a great extent formed by them, in turn playing a part in their formation.

A really adequate phenomenology, and phenomenological sociology, of art, then, operates from the perspective of the *total* world—Husserl's Lebenswelt—of the individual. At a later stage the possibility will have to be considered of extending this to a notion of a total *social* world—that is, the total ideology or Weltanschauung of a

9

social group, rather than an individual (chapter 4). Having here briefly sketched the form which a sociology of art and literature might profitably take, I want to go on to examine the constitutive factors of knowledge in general, beginning with the phenomenological analysis of the Lebenswelt, with reference in particular to Husserl and Merleau-Ponty. This will lead directly into a statement of the essentially *social* nature of the Lebenswelt (already hinted at above), although one ought to note that not all philosophers have taken this step in the argument. At this point, the phenomenology of existence meets the sociology of knowledge, for both take as their premiss the constitution of consciousness in social (as well as non-social) experience. And the sociology of art, as a special branch of the sociology of knowledge, is re-defined as a phenomenology of artistic consciousness.

2 The constitution of knowledge

The sociology of knowledge of Marx, Mannheim and Durkheim, its acknowledged founders, as well as the versions of most other writers on the subject, despite the crucial insights into the relation of thought and socio-economic life, remained at a crude level in certain respects. I am not here referring merely to the simplicity of their various models—to the fact that class is not the only determinant of ideology, for example, and that Mannheim's introduction of generation as an added dimension hardly does more justice to the complexity of the problem. The refinements I consider necessary concern the nature and composition of knowledge itself. My argument is that one cannot divorce the sociology of knowledge from epistemology, that is, from the philosophical theory of knowledge. This contention, I realise, goes against the accepted tenets of sociological theory, at least in England and the United States, which recognises the relevance of philosophy to its own subject-matter only in so far as it restricts itself to what is known as the 'philosophy of (social) science'—that is, methodology, and theoretical self-consciousness. I do not think such a clear demarcation can be, or ought to be, made. What *is* important, of course, is that the type of question being asked is recognised: whether it is empirical, conceptual, theoretical or metaphysical. But I maintain that the investigation of the *nature* of knowledge is at least relevant, and perhaps essential, to both sociological theory and the sociology of knowledge. (I shall argue, further, that other strictly differentiated zones of enquiry are more closely interconnected than is generally accepted. Within sociology itself, sociological theory, methodology, and the sociology of knowledge are, as I have already intimated, interdependent. Sociology, too, involves philosophy; not only epistemology, as I am arguing here, but also, and much more radically, ontology—the philosophy of being. This last contentious point will be raised in a

11

later chapter, when we discuss in greater detail the questions of realism versus idealism, and relativity.)

In the belief, then, that the sociological approach to knowledge presupposes a conception and understanding *of* knowledge, I begin by looking at a number of important philosophical analyses of the genesis and nature of all knowledge of the world (including ideological, evaluative, cognitive, religious, affective). As will become clear, however, philosophical psychology is as dependent on philosophical sociology as I have argued the reverse is the case. In the framework of a phenomenology of mind, the limitations of pure phenomenology and the demand for an inter-subjective perspective quickly become apparent. I have chosen three main topics for consideration here, in anticipation of a subsequent concentration on the sociology of knowledge proper. These are: (i) the phenomenology of knowledge and the social construction of the world; (ii) language and knowledge of the world; and (iii) knowledge and interest—ideology.

i   The phenomenology of knowledge and the social construction of the world

The Lebenswelt, according to Spiegelberg's selective glossary of phenomenological terms, in the index of his two-volume work, *The phenomenological movement* (1960a), is the 'life-world; the encompassing world of our immediate experience which can be recovered from the world as given to scientific interpretation by a special type of reduction' (p. 720). It is particularly important in the theories of the later Husserl and of Merleau-Ponty, and it is in this concept of the Lebenswelt that the philosophies of phenomenology and existentialism coincide. The history of what may rather broadly be termed phenomenological theory, through its major exponents, has been well documented and summarised by Spiegelberg (op. cit.), Thevenaz (1962) and others. Husserl, Heidegger, Sartre and Merleau-Ponty stand out as the major contributors to the movement, and the points at which they confirm, refute and diverge from one another are fully documented in these texts. A very brief summary of this will help to establish the theoretical background of those concepts of existential-phenomenology which are most relevant here.

Spiegelberg's 'minimum list of propositions' defining Husserl's phenomenology will serve as a suitable starting point. He says (1960b):

1. Phenomenology is a rigorous science in the sense of a coherent system of propositions; it goes even beyond positive science by aiming at absolute certainty for its foundations and at freedom from presuppositions that have not passed phenomenological scrutiny.

2. Its subject-matter is the general essences of the phenomena of consciousness; among these phenomena, the phenomenologist distinguishes between the intending acts and the intended objects in strict parallel; he pays special attention to the modes of appearance in which the intended referents present themselves; he does not impose any limitations as to the content of these phenomena.

3. Phenomenology is based on the intuitive exploration and faithful description of the phenomena within the context of the world of our lived experience (*Lebenswelt*), anxious to avoid reductionist over-simplifications and over-complications by preconceived theoretical patterns.

4. In order to secure the fullest possible range of phenomena and at the same time doubt-proof foundations it uses a special method of reductions which suspends the beliefs associated with our naive or natural attitude and shared even by science; it also traces back the phenomena to the constituting acts in a pure subject, which itself proves to be irreducible.

5. Its ultimate objective is the examination and justification of all our beliefs, both ordinary and scientific, by the test of intuitive perception.

As a theory of knowledge, phenomenology returns to the Cartesian premiss which asserts that the only true knowledge we have is of the Cogito. Unlike Descartes, however, Husserl does not rebuild an epistemology based on theology. The second, positive, part of Descartes's method is, of course, a failure in its attempt to reinstate our sure knowledge of the world and of one another (see chapter 3 (ii)). Phenomenology sets about this task without abandoning the original premiss, and knowledge of everything is thus always an aspect of knowledge of the phenomena of consciousness. The self is grasped as a transcendental subjectivity, and as the origin of all meanings. Heidegger extended epistemology into ontology, for he maintained that phenomenology requires a theory of being. His concern is with the *meaning* of being, and not simply the transcendental phenomenology of Husserl. His concept of Dasein, or human existence, as Thevenaz points out, is ontological rather than anthropological; that is, it is not man's *factual* existence which is at issue, but the fundamental structures of being itself.

Sartre also moves from phenomenology to the philosophy of existence, but not as far as the ontology of being. The main distinguishing characteristic of Sartre's theory in relation to Husserl's is his conception of consciousness, which he argues is *not* transcendental. Consciousness is always *of* something; it is always concrete human existence in a human world. 'Being-in-the-world' is implicitly contained in the phenomenological method. (It should be noted, however, that both Heidegger and Sartre abandon the rigorous standards of the phenomenological method in supplementing its deficiencies. See Spiegelberg 1960a, b.)

Finally, the philosophy of Merleau-Ponty unites elements of all three writers. Without sacrificing the strict requirements of phenomenological rigour, he agrees with Sartre that consciousness is 'never suspended in nothingness'. The aim is not, then, withdrawal from the world towards pure consciousness. For Merleau-Ponty, it is the world itself which is primary (unlike Heidegger, for whom being is primary, and Sartre, for whom consciousness is primary). As Thevenaz puts it, the true transcendental is the world—not the external world of traditional philosophy, but the existential relationship of man to the world. The Being-in-the-world of Heidegger is thus made the goal of the Husserlian reduction.

What is often overlooked is the congruence of Merleau-Ponty's theory with certain ideas in Husserl's later work, particularly in *The crisis of the European sciences and transcendental phenomenology*. Spiegelberg (1960b) suggests that Husserl was aware of the problems of 'so-called "existence"', objecting only to 'the claim to priority of the existential analytics over his own transcendental phenomenology, which Heidegger had implied'. The concept of the Lebenswelt, which appears only in Husserl's last writings, opens the way to the realisation of the existential possibilities of the phenomenological method. The Lebenswelt is the world of lived experience, the general context in which each particular experience and perception occurs, and through which it finds its meaning. The difference between a phenomenology which takes the Lebenswelt as its point of reference, and one which examines phenomena in isolation, is clear in Spiegelberg's account of Husserl's own progression from the latter to the former (1960a, p. 161).

> His earlier phenomenological studies in the field of perception and of other intentional acts had focussed only on specific and isolated phenomena. Nevertheless, largely under the stimulation of William James, Husserl had always been aware of the significance of 'fringes', or, as he mostly called them, 'horizons', for the phenomena as essential features of their make-up.
> But only gradually he came to see that even these horizons were not merely open areas of decreasing clarity, but parts of the comprehensive horizon of a world as their encompassing frame of reference, without which any account of even a single perception would be incomplete.

The similarity of this perspective with Gestalt theory is plain, and, indeed, is made explicit by Merleau-Ponty. For example, with reference to the phenomenology of perception, he says (1967, pp. 48–9):

> It is precisely Gestalt psychology which has brought home to us the tensions which run like lines of force across the visual field and the system constituted by my own body and the world, and which breathe into it a secret and magic life by exerting here and there forces of distortion, contraction and expansion.

He goes on to criticise Gestalt psychologists for not taking their argument to its real conclusion, and for remaining within the old naturalism of explanatory psychology, which looks for the external *causes* of phenomena, instead of internal 'motives' (p. 49).

> What Gestalt psychology lacks . . . is a set of new categories: it has admitted the principle, and applied it to a few individual cases, but without realizing that a complete reform of understanding is called for if we are to translate phenomena accurately; and that to this end the objective thinking of classical logic and philosophy will have to be questioned, the categories of the world laid aside, the alleged self-evidence of realism placed in doubt, in the Cartesian sense, and a true 'phenomenological reduction' undertaken.

Merleau-Ponty's phenomenology, like Gestalt psychology, rejects psychological atomism, but proceeds to show that this is 'only one particular case of a more general prejudice; the prejudice of determinate being or of the world' (ibid., p. 51 n.). When this is recognised —that is, when Gestalt theory becomes existential-phenomenology— 'the world, which I distinguished from myself as the totality of things or of processes linked by causal relationships, I rediscover "in me" as the permanent horizon of all my *cogitationes* and as a dimension in relation to which I am constantly situating myself' (ibid., Preface, p. xiii).

The crucial premiss of the philosophy of the Lebenswelt is that of the structuredness of any experience, and the unity of the Lebenswelt, and it is this which will prove essential to an existentially-orientated sociology of art and aesthetics. To quote Merleau-Ponty again (ibid., p. 407):

> I am not myself a succession of 'psychic' acts, nor for that matter a nuclear *I* who bring them together into a synthetic unity, but one single experience inseparable from itself, one single 'living cohesion', one single temporality which is engaged, from birth, in making itself progressively explicit, and in confirming that cohesion in each successive present.

15

It is in the context of this I, and of this experiential unity, that any new experience, perception or sensation finds its meaning.

Alfred Schutz, taking as his starting-point, like Merleau-Ponty, the insights of Husserl, explains the nature of the Lebenswelt and its relation to the particular spheres of experience ('Phenomenology and the social sciences', 1967, pp. 134–6).

> This world, built around my own I, presents itself for interpretation to me, a being living naively within it. From this standpoint everything has reference to my actual historical situation, or as we can also say, to my pragmatic interests which belong to the situation in which I find myself here and now ... [The naive person] posits this world in a 'general thesis' as meaningfully valid for him, with all that he finds in it, with all natural things, with all living beings (especially with human beings), and with meaningful products of all sorts (tools, symbols, language systems, works of art, etc.). Hence, the naively living person (we are speaking of healthy, grown-up, and wide-awake human beings) automatically has in hand, so to speak, the meaningful complexes which are valid for him. From things inherited and learned, from the manifold sedimentations of tradition, habituality, and his own previous constitutions of meaning, which can be retained and reactivated, his *store of experience* of his life-world is built-up as a closed meaningful complex.

Elsewhere, Schutz discusses scientific thought, as one mode of experience grounded, like all other possible modes, in the natural attitude of the life-world ('Concept and theory formation', pp. 57–8).

> The common-sense knowledge of everyday life is the unquestioned but always questionable back-ground within which inquiry starts and within which alone it can be carried out. It is this *Lebenswelt*, as Husserl calls it, within which, according to him, all scientific and even logical concepts originate. .... The concept of Nature ... with which the natural sciences have to deal is, as Husserl has shown, an idealizing abstraction from the *Lebenswelt*.

And, it can be added, artistic, religious, mythological and other forms of knowledge similarly have their origin in the life-world.

It is important to see that this is *not* a contingent fact, but an essential feature of experience. Phenomenology reveals the total, meaningful world of lived experience, and at the same time discloses this as the primary existential reality. Experience, inasmuch as it is meaningful to the experiencer, is necessarily interpreted in the context of his existing life-world. As Natanson puts it (1967, p. xxviii):

16

the funded experience of a life, what a phenomenologist would
call the 'sedimented' structure of the individual's experience,
is the condition for the subsequent interpretation of all new
events and activities.

This is clearly of great importance for the psychology of perception,
and, indeed, for psychology as a whole. (This, of course, is the
central tenet of existential-phenomenological psychologists and
psychiatrists, in the critique of traditional schools of psychology;
e.g. R. D. Laing, Rollo May, Eugene Minkowski, as well as Gestalt
theorists.) More relevant here, however, are the inferences to be
drawn for aesthetics and the sociology of art. Since the experience
and creation of works of art are one part of the total life-world,
they must find both their origin and their meaning within this world.
A proper comprehension of art as a mode of experience (a 'reality')
and of art in society, will therefore be in terms of the Lebenswelt
of the individuals concerned in its creation and appreciation.

The Lebenswelt is, furthermore, a *social* world. This argument was
not developed by Husserl, although his later writings, introducing
the concept of 'inter-subjectivity', point in that direction, and were
followed up by later writers. Merleau-Ponty, for example, affirms
the social nature of individual knowledge (see, for example, Merleau-
Ponty 1951, p. 65). It is Schutz who demonstrates this most fully,
and it is in his work that phenomenology and sociology meet. I shall
examine his arguments in a moment, but first I want to make clear
what I mean by the social nature of the Lebenswelt. There are two
ways in which the life-world is a social world. First, the meanings
the world has for the individual, in so far as they are *learned* meanings, acquired in social interaction and socialisation, are pre-
existing *social* meanings. Second, the individual is not alone in
this life-world, but shares it with his fellow men, and in this sense,
too, it is a 'social' world. The second proposition is related to, and
in fact is a corollary of, the first, and it will be considered more
closely in a later chapter, when we come to the problem of the
Weltanschauung. It is the first definition of the social nature of the
Lebenswelt which I am concerned with here. As Schutz has shown,
this is not only a valid extension of the phenomenology of the
Lebenswelt; it is an essential feature of it ('Concept and theory
formation', p. 61; see also 'Common-sense and scientific interpretation', pp. 13–14).

The common-sense knowledge of everyday life is from the
outset . . . genetically socialized, because the greater part of our
knowledge, as to its content and the particular forms of
typification under which it is organized, is socially derived, and
this in socially approved terms.

17

The phenomenology of mind is certainly right in taking as its primary
data the phenomena *of* mind in isolation, and not the scientific
concept of mental phenomena, logical constructs or theoretical
abstractions from our (non-phenomenological) knowledge of the
world. But as soon as it attempts to deal with the phenomenological
constitution of the Lebenswelt—that is, the origin of mental facts,
as opposed to their simple examination—its inter-subjective, or
social, nature becomes apparent ('Phenomenology and the social
sciences', p. 121).

> My transcendental subjectivity, in the activities of which this
> world is constituted, must thus from the beginning be related
> to other subjectivities, in relation to the activities of which it
> authorizes and rectifies its own.

This, then, is the meeting point of phenomenology and the
sociology of knowledge. It might be argued that the sociology of
knowledge, thus proved to have a sound epistemological foundation,
is at the same time left unaffected by the above discussion and
that this discussion neither contributes anything new to the sociology
of knowledge (and thus to the sociology of art) nor forces any
critical re-evaluation of its premisses and procedures, and is thus
superfluous. But although, as I have stated earlier, the sociology of
art *can* proceed without the phenomenological self-consciousness I
have been advocating (just as the natural sciences can, and indeed
must, proceed without it), the point of my argument is that such an
awareness must prove extremely valuable to the sociologist. It will
enable him to understand elements of the culture he is studying
which may on the surface seem idiosyncratic and meaningless, and
it will suggest to him where to look for relevant information in a
new area of investigation. The sociology of art will not, then, more
or less arbitrarily choose another social fact (class, religion, etc.)
with which to correlate styles of art or amount of creativity, but, in
understanding art in its total context of a meaningful world, should
expose its relations to any other aspects of that world which are
relevant.

Among sociologists, it is primarily Berger and Luckmann who,
following Schutz, make explicit the phenomenological foundation
of the premiss that knowledge is socially derived (Berger and Luckmann 1967). They open the first chapter of their book with the
following statement (p. 13): 'The basic contentions of the argument of
this book are ... that reality is socially constructed and that the
sociology of knowledge must analyse the process in which this
occurs.' They go on to examine and analyse the processes by which
the individual acquires knowledge in society, namely internalisation
(or socialisation), by which society becomes subjective reality,

externalisation and objectivation (institutionalisation), by which it becomes objective reality. Although they insist that the sociology of knowledge 'must concern itself with everything that passes for "knowledge" in society' (p. 26), criticising earlier theorists who limited themselves to what Berger and Luckmann call 'the sphere of ideas, that is of theoretical thought' (p. 24), they themselves produce a specific sociology of knowledge, namely a sociology of *social* knowledge. They succeed in extending the discipline to include the commonsense knowledge of the ordinary man, but consider only his knowledge about society itself, and about the roles, institutions and legitimating ideology, or Weltanschauung, of social life. Clearly this is a fundamental form of knowledge, but it seems that Berger and Luckmann consider other forms of knowledge to be derivative from it. If this is indeed their view, I think it is mistaken. Symbolic universes are not *just* legitimating ideologies, arising from the need to justify the originally arbitrary, and therefore precarious, structure of social life. They are not even merely symbolic legitimations for an opposition to the existing social structure and the defence of an alternative society. A sociology of symbolic systems will need to develop a more subtle line of approach to what are extremely complex problems.

Nevertheless, I would contend that Berger and Luckmann's analysis *can* be extended into other branches of the sociology of knowledge. (Berger (1967) himself has applied similar arguments in the field of religion, in his book *The sacred canopy: elements of a sociological theory of religion*.) The crucial insight is into the *social* construction of reality. In the context of art and literature, too, the 'knowledge' is a social phenomenon in the same sense. Furthermore, as I have argued, artistic knowledge is a part of a *total* knowledge of reality, a coherent Lebenswelt. A phenomenological sociology of art will take into account both these facts. It will comprehend the meanings in art in terms of the wider cultural system, and it will at the same time make clear the social aspect of an ostensibly individual creation. This, incidentally, deals neatly with the problem of psychology versus sociology of art. Since the individual's reality is itself social, in the way I have shown, then social factors will enter into even a psychology of art (or of anything else). Thus, even before we discuss the possibility of moving from the individual to the social group, as the repository of meanings, the social nature of meanings in art is evident.

ii Language and knowledge of the world

In this section, I want to consider the question of the extent to which a sociology of knowledge involves a sociology of language.

19

Here, we remain on the level of the social individual for it is on this level that the role of language in experience must be explicated, before knowledge of social groups can be discussed. As I will show, a strong case for the necessity for a linguistically-orientated approach to philosophy and the cultural sciences has been put forward by philosophers, psychologists, linguists and sociologists, and it is important to determine the validity of this claim, and to discover the extent to which, and the manner in which, linguistics plays a part in a verstehende sociology.

Habermas (1970) maintains that the methodology of Verstehen-sociology and the phenomenological approach are inadequate for a proper sociological understanding of the subject-matter. Like Weber, Schutz, Cicourel, Garfinkel and others, he insists on the centrality of 'meaning' in human action and therefore of the role of understanding in the human sciences. Unlike them, he is not satisfied with a phenomenological penetration of the actor's Lebenswelt, or some more mysterious (at least undefined) empathic grasp of the actor's situation, complete with its meanings and significances for him, perhaps by some kind of generalisation of the sociologist's own experience. Transcendental contemplation, as firmly grounded and presuppositionless as the phenomena (following Husserl's precepts) may be, in the field of sociology can be no substitute for systematic participation (p. 215).

> We only grasp the construction of individual life-worlds by way of
> socially accustomed communications; but one learns their
> specified rules by systematic participation and not, as Schutz
> assumes, by phenomenological intuition, or as Cicourel and
> Garfinkel assume, by phenomenologically guided experiments.

And the factor overlooked by transcendental phenomenology, and essential for true Verstehen, is language. Here, Habermas seems to have a number of reasons for emphasising the need for a socio-linguistic approach, although he does not present them as distinct arguments, nor does he appear to differentiate them in this section of his book. They may be summarised as follows:

a The 'definition of the situation', of which, it is agreed, the sociologist will take account, is itself interpreted by the actor in terms of his *communication* with his consociates. Thus Garfinkel must leave phenomenology and enter the field of linguistics, argues Habermas (p. 214): 'He would then be able to grasp those rules of interpretation according to which the actor defines his situation and his self-understanding, as what they are—as rules of action—directing communication.'

b The sociologist needs to communicate with his subject in order to understand him; this communication is, of course, through spoken language.

c Action (of the subject) is itself inextricably bound up with language (Wittgenstein's argument).

d Intentions, etc. derive, in part at least, from linguistic meanings. 'The nexus of intentions, on which the investigation of intentional action falls, will no longer be clarified by a transcendental genesis of "meaning" (*Sinn*), but by a logical analysis of linguistic meanings (*sprachlichen Bedeutungen*)' (p. 221).

e Wittgenstein's argument, that the view of the world is reflected in the rules of speech. (Habermas quotes Wittgenstein's *Philosophical Investigations* 54.)

Habermas's own discussion, and in some cases critique, of these points need not be elaborated here. More importantly, his conclusion, and his chief criticism of the Weber–Schutz approach to sociology, is that to understand *meaning*, we must understand *language*.

Habermas is not directly concerned with problems of the sociology of knowledge, at least in this work. The central issue is not that of how social consciousness and individual perspectives arise and in what phenomena their roots lie, but rather it is one of the methodology of the social sciences themselves; the question is, how can the sociologist get to that consciousness and perspective, and what are the precepts he must follow in order to understand and describe them adequately? However, if Habermas's arguments are valid, they may be shown to have important consequences for the sociology of knowledge. The question I want to consider, therefore, is to what extent (if at all) the sociologist must enter the field of linguistics when he is primarily concerned with *other* forms of 'knowledge' (in the sense of 'the sociology of knowledge'). This entails a discussion of the nature of language itself, of its role in social life and personal experience, and its relationship to other cultural systems.

Language, it is claimed, is one of the primary factors in structuring thought (and, it is sometimes added, in limiting it). Much has been written on the sociology of language (for example, Bernstein's work on the relationship between social class and language usage; Hertzler's (1965) book, *A sociology of language*, summarises much of the literature), but for reasons which I will attempt to justify here, I want to limit my discussion of the topic to a somewhat narrow section of the vast subject of the relation between language and social life. In another way, I shall be extending the subject in a direction which, in strict terms, leads out of sociology proper and into psychology and philosophy. This I consider essential because I feel that the influence of language on thought and perception—that is, on the immediate content of human experience, before we get to the level of *social* interaction and *inter*-subjective experience—is a question

21

which is central to the whole problem. Furthermore, I do not consider that there is any contradiction between this view and the argument that *any* kind of human experience *presupposes* social existence. It may be true, as Mead was one of the first to argue, that one's definition of the self, the pre-condition for all self-conscious experience, arises only in the social situation, and that only *inter*action gives rise to non-instinctive action, intelligent behaviour, expectations and thus the individual consciousness itself. Nevertheless, granted that individuals are necessarily socially defined and created, and also that language itself is necessarily a social product, it is profitable to start, as phenomenology does, from the perspective of the individual, taking language as a *fact*, and to enquire as to the interaction between these two, putting to one side the social dimension. (Indeed, most of the work to be mentioned in this respect has been done by phenomenologists.) This is by no means anti-sociological. It is hoped that such an analysis, in conjunction with analyses of the more sociological questions involved, such as the social nature of language, the social determinants of thought, through language, etc., will be able to lead to some attempt to answer the main question we are considering here, before we can go on to use these results in wider considerations in the sociology of culture.

That language is necessarily a social phenomenon need not be argued here; I mention the point merely to state that I take this for granted. Another interesting and more philosophical question which again I shall not discuss here, is the debate about the claim that the necessity for language to be social is a *logical* necessity (Wittgenstein 1963; Winch 1971). Neither do I propose to discuss the much-debated issue of the origin of language, its development from pre-linguistic forms of communication and the significance of its appearance in the history of man's evolution. Modern linguists, not only those concerned with formal problems of structure, but also those concerned with the dynamics of change in language, have long since given up such speculative studies.

Of recent work in the sociology of language, there are also certain questions which have been discussed which are only marginally relevant to our interests. Hertzler (1965) discusses language as an agency of social control, as a socio-cultural index and record (for example, names of people and places), in its role in propaganda, in its unifying and dividing effects among societies (in terms of facilitating communication, for example). All of these can be listed among the social aspects of language, but their consideration does not, I feel, help to answer the more basic question of the place of language in thought and experience. Bernstein's writings, which are apparently concerned with a more specific problem than ours, in fact are more relevant than other attemps to correlate dialect, styles of speech, etc., with social situation. Such data, as long as they remain on the level of, on the one hand, linguistic analysis (whether of style, grammar or phonetics), will not, without further related research, tell us much about the importance of language, limited and determined as it may be by social factors, for any other, more fundamental, aspects of its users' lives, outlooks and cultural characteristics. Bernstein does go further than this, when he demonstrates the *effects* of different ways of speaking on intellectual ability and learning. Others have undertaken similar studies; they suggest that the language we use is an important determining influence on other intellectual capabilities, such as our ability to grasp abstract ideas, to think logically, etc.

Far more radical theories on these lines are those which are usually called theories of 'linguistic relativity'. The so-called Sapir–Whorf hypothesis has been the subject of a multitude of articles, both providing empirical evidence in support of the hypothesis, and putting forward empirical and theoretical evidence attacking it. It has also been the focus of at least one conference (Hoijer 1954), and of sections of a number of anthologies (Henle 1965, chapter 1; Hymes 1964, part III). The hypothesis, briefly, argues that the individual's total experience, including perception, ways of thinking, view of the world, is moulded by his language. As Sapir puts it, 'Every experience is saturated with verbalism' ('Language', in Sapir 1966, p. 9). And, as languages exist within social communities of speakers, he also claims that the worlds in which different societies live are distinct worlds. Whorf, a pupil of Sapir, and the writer, who, of the two, is more usually considered the chief exponent of this hypothesis, wrote in a much-quoted essay ('Science and linguistics', 1967, p. 214):

> We are thus introduced to a new principle of relativity, which holds that all observers are not led by the same physical evidence to the same picture of the universe, unless their linguistic backgrounds are similar, or can in some way be calibrated.

In support of his hypothesis, Whorf uses his detailed knowledge of American Indian languages, in particular Hopi, and attempts to show a parallel relationship of language structure to world-view in the cases of these languages and in Standard Average European (SAE) languages. Thus he shows how, in Hopi, a lack of tenses in verb forms is connected with a conception of time entirely alien to a European speaker ('An American Indian model of the universe', 1967). Other examples are also given and purport to account for what appear to the observer to be strange views of the world, society and of man's place in both. Followers of Whorf offer results of their own researches in linguistic anthropology, apparently confirming the

23

linguistic relativity hypothesis. Hoijer (1951), for example, provides what Hymes considers one of the best documented and soundest studies, linking grammar (as one aspect of language) with culture. Dorothy Lee, in a series of articles, which are not primarily concerned with language as such, subscribes to the view that 'reality'—i.e. the world as it appears to man—is determined by cultural situation, including language, and uses her knowledge of Greek and American Indian, especially Wintu, cultures to make the point. 'Culture is a symbolic system which transforms the physical reality, what is *there*, into experienced reality' (Lee 1959, p. 1).

Here, some criticisms of Whorf's theory by other linguists might be considered. Roger Brown argues that Whorf *assumes* the hypothesis in his very method of investigation, since it is by no means obvious that the grouping of European languages into one category (SAE) is any more legitimate than differentiating, say, Hopi *from* SAE. There *are* differences in style, grammatical structure, ways of describing a situation, etc., between English and German, for example. (Brown quotes Mark Twain's literal translation of a German speech into English, to show that translation between these languages requires some degree of flexibility, if we are to get across the *meaning* of what is said.) Whorf's prejudice, claims Brown, lies in not questioning 'free translation' between SAE languages, while refusing to translate freely from Hopi to English (R. Brown 1958). This is hardly damaging to the hypothesis, however. Whorf did, it is true, take as identical, for his purposes, languages in what he called the SAE group, but there would have been no reason, if his interest had been primarily in *these* languages rather than the Indian languages, why he might not have applied his hypothesis to several of the European languages too. The point, indeed, is that SAE languages have far more in common (and, *ex hypothesi*, their related cultural outlooks have more in common) with one another than any one of them does with Hopi, and this is what makes a comparison of Hopi and English so much more revealing and rewarding.

Another line of attack, once considered fatal to Whorf's theory, runs parallel to that so often used against Mannheim's sociology of knowledge (see chapter 3 (i)). This concerns the vicious circle involved in any theories of relativity of knowledge. In this case, the argument is that if linguistic relativity were true, cross-cultural studies would be impossible, since any potential investigator is himself culture-bound, and prevented by his own linguistic (and other) framework from entering that of another society. Indeed, it seems that cultural and linguistic studies in one's *own* society become impossible, as some degree of objectivity, of looking at the phenomena at a distance, is essential even in *describing* those phenomena. (Besides a number of linguists, Habermas has also used this criticism against Wittgenstein and others, attempting to solve the problem by an appeal to hermeneutics, as propounded principally by Gadamer.) Now the argument seems to be more or less accepted, but not necessarily felt to be damaging to the relativity hypothesis; writers accept that a thesis of *absolute* relativity is impossible to maintain, and the hypothesis is accordingly modified, to include certain cross-cultural 'universals', to grant that linguistic determinism itself is not absolute, or to provide for some means of inter-cultural translation, both of languages and of non-linguistic features.

More technical complaints concern the necessity to be more explicit about what is meant by 'language' in this context. Is it grammar, lexical categories, structure, or semantics, which, allegedly, codes and defines 'reality'? Such questions are discussed by Greenberg (in Hoijer 1954), Henle (1965), Hoijer (in Hoijer 1954) and Newman (in Hoijer 1954). No general conclusion has been reached that any of these levels of linguistic analysis is to be taken as the crucial one, although perhaps a reasonable conclusion one may draw from these papers and a number of others, is that some consensus appears to exist, to the effect that *purely* structural (phonetic, phonemic, morphemic, grammatical or lexical) analysis, to the exclusion of semantic considerations, is liable to make unnecessary errors. (See, for example, the discussion between D. W. Brown and Rapoport, D. W. Brown 1960.) A structural feature with no semantic correlate might, at best, signify an obsolete cultural fact. To give just one example of this important point, Hockett (in Hoijer 1954) shows that the Chinese word for 'train', which literally means 'fire-cart', no longer *means* 'fire-cart'; to put this in another way, the Chinese word for a train conveys or names exactly the same concept as does 'train' in English, whatever may have been the case when the name was originally coined. The general argument illustrated is, I feel, unquestionably a valid one. Whether or not one can go beyond this, to maintain that semantics *alone* can provide the key to cultural and mental phenomena, while formal linguistics remains totally irrelevant, is, of course, another question.

Those problems which are essentially purely internal to the field of linguistics are rather beside the point of this chapter. From the literature on linguistics, we can simply note a number of useful and suggestive facts; for example, the fact that, at the lexical level, there is an acknowledged correlation between the existence of words and the differentiation of separate words in a group, and the social and environmental conditions of the speakers of the language. (Two of the best-known examples of this are the fact that the Eskimos have a variety of names for different types of snow, all covered by one word in English; and, conversely, that one word, for certain desert tribes, includes all flying things, from birds to aeroplanes.) We

can also take account of Whorf's and others' suggestions that grammar and style of speech indicate certain conceptions of self, time,
society and reality, without actually committing ourselves to the
linguistic relativity hypothesis, in the form in which Whorf, Carroll
or any of the subsequent writers proposing modified forms of the
hypothesis have stated it. (Some have preferred to say that language,
rather than determining and confining the possibilities of experience,
merely facilitates certain experiential phenomena and discourages
others; see Henle 1965; Hoijer 1953. This is confirmed by empirical
studies on the relation of colour vocabulary to colour perception.)
Bearing in mind all these suggestions, the line I want to pursue is that
of a phenomenological study of the role of language in thought and
experience.

The conclusions of phenomenologists of language have also been
reached independently by other philosophers. The nineteenth-
century German writer, Humboldt, who was the first to expound
the theory of linguistic relativity, wrote (quoted by Cassirer 1953,
p. 9):

> Man lives with his objects chiefly—in fact, since his feeling and
> acting depends on his perceptions, one may say exclusively—as
> language presents them to him. By the same process whereby
> he spins language out of his own being, he ensnares himself in
> it; and each language draws a magic circle round the people to
> which it belongs, a circle from which there is no escape save
> by stepping out of it into another.

In much the same tradition, Baudouin de Courtenay has written more
recently, arguing that the world exists in the mind as a dictionary
('die Welt existiert in menschlicher Seele als ein Wörterbuch, oder
vielmehr als viele verschiedensprachige Wörterbücher', de Courtenay
1929, p. 203). This, surely, is the extreme of the claim that 'reality'
is a linguistic creation. The Weltanschauung of speech, he claims,
becomes that of man. The problem of what speech *is*, how *its*
Weltanschauung arose, is answered, rather unsatisfactorily, by saying
that language developed to mirror differences in nature, society and
psychology; once developed, it exercises its influence, colouring
perception and experience. I say this is unsatisfactory because although it might appear to make some attempt to give the necessary
(as I would argue) dynamic view of the nature of language, in fact
all it does is present a far from convincing early history of language
as a starting point, and proceed to take language as static. At the
same time, however, it allows a more complex and interesting conception to emerge, namely the idea that language and experience are
mutually influential, and in some way interact. The stress of the
essay is on the one-way relationship of language-to-perception, and

this, provided it is clear that we know we are taking a one-sided approach, is perfectly in order. My criticism is that Baudouin de Courtenay seems to think he is giving a complete analysis; he raises the question 'which comes first, language or perception?', and the pseudo-dynamic model he presents is his answer. The rest of his article consists of extremely weak illustrations of his argument, mainly concerned with the role of gender in language, and its influence on thought. His general thesis, however, remains acceptable, even if not proved: 'We have the right to suppose that the diversity of the morphological structure of languages is not without a certain influence on the world-view of the speakers of that language' (p. 206).

The rather speculative theories of these and other writers are in fact supported by the empirical results of experimental psychology. For example, Brown and Lenneberg (1954) have shown that the availability of a large number of colour-concepts enhances ability to recognise and identify particular colours, by demonstrating that a sample of college women, used in an experiment, named colours to themselves when they were presented with them, in order to help them in recognising the colours later in a chart of 120 colours. Another experiment by Lenneberg and Roberts (1956) on these lines, supported the conclusion that colour codability and colour recognition are related. It was shown that, in comparing English-speaking and Zuni-speaking subjects, differences in codability were reflected by parallel differences in ability to recognise and remember colours. Other experiments show how the *name* which a figure is given by the investigator influences the subject's perception of it (Carmichael, Hogan and Walter, 1932). Finally, in an experiment by Carroll and Casagrande (1958), English-speaking and Navaho-speaking children were compared in their use of shape, form or material, rather than colour, as a basis for sorting objects. It was found that Navaho-speaking children performed sorting tasks on the basis of form at younger ages than English-speaking children; this difference was traced to differences in grammar between the two languages, Navaho placing greater stress on shapes and forms. On the basis of these and similar experiments, Carroll concludes: 'The important role of verbal mediators in behavior is so well attested that it can hardly be denied' (Carroll 1964, p. 98), behaviour being seen as response to stimuli, whose perception, it is claimed, is mediated by the language and concepts acquired by the actor.

The question, of course, is *why* this is so; how is it that language can structure thought and experience, and in what way does this occur? This cannot be answered by linguists, anthropologists or psychologists, and it is now time to consider the question from the perspective of the earlier part of this book.

27

As I have argued above, reality is socially constituted. This applies not only to subjective reality, but also to objective reality—that is, to those aspects of our world which we do not feel to be personal interpretations or perspectives, but which are communally confirmed, and accepted as in some sense 'real' independently of the observer. It should be made clear that 'reality' here means more than just the world of physical, observable objects and events (and I would argue that even these are interpreted rather than directly experienced in their immediacy, and that this interpretation is largely social in origin); 'reality' covers also those cultural facts which are regarded as 'existing', as something 'there', apart from any contemporary action or interaction, and as something taken into account by the actor, as an objectivity. This, it should be noted, applies not only when such a cultural fact, institution or product has been reified, but as soon as it is accepted as a pre-existing background to action, rather than regarded still as something to be modified *by* social action; in other words, as soon as it is institutionalised. It is in this sense that Berger and Luckmann (1967) discuss 'reality', although, as I have already mentioned, they do so in the limited area of *social* reality (knowledge about society). But in all areas of knowledge, what we take as objective is in fact what is handed down in the socialisation process *as* objective. As Berger and Luckmann show, the construction of reality is a *social* phenomenon.

A fundamental prejudice inclines those unfamiliar with this philosophical approach, essentially Kantian, to ask why reality cannot be absolute, and, as such, immediately perceived. At least, it might be argued, we may grant those phenomena which are clearly social in origin—institutions and other cultural facts—are 'real' only by virtue of a conventional definition, but nevertheless *non*-cultural events and objects are 'real' in an absolute sense. We cannot deny the objective reality and existence of a person, a stone or a collision. The prejudice, of course, is nothing but commitment to the axioms of the scientific method; metaphysics questions these axioms themselves, and concludes that, not only is it impossible to prove the existence of certain things-in-themselves, with observable characteristics (phenomenalism, for example, is a perfectly plausible doctrine), but that it is hard to see how it even makes sense to talk about 'absolute reality'. In Kant's terms, we can neither know nor theorise about the noumena, supposedly underlying the phenomena of experience. The initial, destructive part of Descartes's critique of knowledge was sound. This, as we have seen above, is the starting point of phenomenology, and this is the epistemological foundation of the case for the inevitable 'subjectivity' of knowledge.[1]

Having sketched briefly the lines a philosophical justification of

[1] This question is discussed in more detail in chapter 3.

the relativity-of-knowledge argument would take, we are brought back immediately to language, and its part in the construction of reality. The obvious point is, of course, that if reality *is* socially defined, and learned in the primary and secondary stages of the socialisation process (Berger and Luckmann), and if it is only through language that we learn at all, a view of reality is dependent on language. The point I prefer to elaborate here is rather more controversial; it is the argument that language, in so far as we take this as given and not in a permanent state of creation and recreation (a methodological, and not a factual, assumption), *of its own accord* structures reality, by virtue of its essential categorisations, emphases and structure. This is to return to the linguistic relativity argument, and here the task will be to examine the hypothesis at a more fundamental level. We can no longer remain content with the theory that language structures experience, and with empirical evidence which supports the claim, but must enquire *how* this can be so, and *how* reality is in fact constructed for the individual. If a sound basis in philosophical psychology can be built, then the prolonged debate at the higher level will become irrelevant, for it will have been shown conclusively that language does (or, on the other hand, does *not*) have a role in structuring reality.

Benda (1959), defining consciousness as the totality of meaningful interpretations of life experience which the individual finds available, argues that this depends on the language into which he is born. 'Reality becomes a meaningful part of consciousness only through a linguistic interpretation of the reality-contact.' This is because a name does not refer to an existing reality, but merely to a *concept*, this representing a *cluster* of images. The world of experience is a world of named objects, and, clearly, the group of images associated with a concept is arbitrary (i.e. could have been otherwise). Thus Benda argues that perception gains configuration and meaning by the conceptual and linguistic significance through which it enters consciousness.

An article by Cassirer (1933) argues the same point. Perception, Cassirer says, is indissolubly linked with language, which is the mediator in the construction of the objective world. Turning round the traditional view of an objective world to be discovered in experience and described in words, he argues that objectivity is the *aim*, rather than the point of departure, of language. An 'object' is experienced by virtue of its *name*, this being a unity formed out of a multiplicity of representations. This is exactly Benda's argument, in slightly different terms. Cassirer expands the same argument in his book, *Language and myth*, where he begins by insisting that symbolic forms (including language) are not imitations, but *organs* of reality. 'It is solely by their agency that anything real becomes an object for intellectual apprehension, and as such is made visible to us' (p. 8). Following an account of the origin of language in mythical thought, he argues, further, that concepts, rather than being copies of a definite world of facts, are distillations of experiences, and it is these which serve to make distinctions and fix them in consciousness.

In a more detailed investigation of this question, Church (1961) discusses in a systematic way the nature of the experience of reality, and the transformation achieved in this by the learning of language. This is seen as making the step from 'primitive' to 'mature' functioning. In becoming a 'verbal organism', the child undergoes an important change, as a result of which language dominates and transforms his *pre*-verbal experience. At the same time, Church disagrees with Whorf as to the degree of domination involved, and emphasises *other* cultural influences on perception and behaviour (for example, unverbalised beliefs). Also, he says, possibilities for 'primitive thought' always continue to exist, even for the adult, in his orientation to reality. (This, I think, means simply that perception *can* be unstructured and outside the scope of social schematisation.) The central contention, however, remains that we can only come to terms with reality through language, and that it is entirely mistaken to believe that we can somehow grasp concrete reality independently of it.

The evidence of psychologists, anthropologists and philosophers thus confirms the hypothesis that reality is (amongst other things) a linguistic creation. But what are the consequences of this for the sociologist? We can say, of course, that commitment to the method of Verstehen entails the necessity to understand his subject's language and style of speech. This is nothing new, however, but is implied by the method itself, as Wittgenstein, Winch and many contemporary sociologists and anthropologists have shown. More than this, it now looks as though a sociological understanding must be preceded by an exhaustive and thorough investigation of language and its structuring influence on thought and experience. Berger and Luckmann certainly did not have such a radical programme in mind when they wrote 'the sociology of knowledge presupposes a sociology of language' (1967, p. 207); for them, language maintains and expresses reality, rather than creating it, and it is because it plays an essential part in everyday life in this way that 'an understanding of language is . . . essential for any understanding of the reality of everyday life' (ibid., pp. 51–2). When we recognise the more fundamental connection of language with the reality of everyday life, it becomes relevant to reconsider the place of sociolinguistics in the sociology of knowledge.

I argued earlier that the sociology of knowledge starts with the phenomenological comprehension of 'knowledge' as the investigation of the Lebenswelt. From this point of view, it is clear that Verstehen does not have to be simply reduced to, or even dependent on, linguistics. The phenomenology of mind, by its very nature, operates on a level far deeper than the empirical study of language. It is true that a phenomenological analysis of the genetic constitution of consciousness will have occasion to refer to the role of language in this (see Cassirer's article, quoted above). But the synchronic analysis of the everyday reality (or of any of the multiple realities) of the mind, which does not need to explain the genesis of that reality, needs no more refer to language than to the rest of the experiential biography of the subject. Moving further, to inter-subjective understanding, the situation is modified. There is no direct access to the phenomena in the way in which there is in pure phenomenology. In this case, access to the Lebenswelt must be, in part at least, through an understanding of its origin and constitution. In other words, we have to be able to place the particular act or experience of the other in the context (implicit and unproblematic in the case of *self*-understanding) of his biographical situation. When Schutz talks about inter-subjective Verstehen in terms of the grasping of typifications, he does not make this point clear. But the typifications must be *relevant*, and their relevance can only be guaranteed by reference to the actor's Lebenswelt, reconstructed by the observer/sociologist through its historical and contemporaneous constituting elements. Language, as we have seen, is one of these elements.

I am inclined to argue that the question raised in the last paragraphs of this section demands a solution only on the theoretical level. In practice, it will be clear to the investigator just how much his subject's language patterns are an independent determining factor in the totality of his life-world. The important point is that the sociologist should retain an open mind towards language as a potential influence, so that where certain behavioural or motivational patterns are incomprehensible in some of their aspects, linguistic factors will not be overlooked. The demands of theoretical sociology, however, are for a more precise definition of the role of sociolinguistics in the sociology of knowledge; the pragmatic approach suggested does not stand up to the requirements of systematic, methodological rigour. On the theoretical level, then, I am afraid I must admit failure, for not only can I not provide a comprehensive account of the method of a sociolinguistic sociology: I believe any attempt to give such an account would be misconceived. Winch (1971), for example, taking this as the essential task for sociology, finishes by reducing the latter to a kind of semantics, and excluding most of what sociology is actually about. Without necessarily following his argument to this extreme, any such *a priori* theorising is more or less bound to hinder the practising sociologist by directing and restricting his vision in a way which, first, may not even produce any information of value, and second, would certainly involve the risk of obscuring or underestimating other equally relevant factors. The method of Verstehen must operate with a sensitivity to language as an element of consciousness, at the same time avoiding the temptation to concentrate too much on this one 'form of life' (Wittgenstein's phrase, used also by Winch). Furthermore (and this, I think, is the crucial point to be made in the face of all the evidence for the formative, structuring effects of language on thought), if motivation, intentionality, modes of thought, etc., are accessible to Verstehen in their own right, the approach through linguistics is superfluous. This is a reiteration of my earlier statement that only where a more direct access to mind is impossible is an analysis of consciousness via its genetic sources (including language) necessary or worthwhile. For example, it may well be true that the animistic, passive, defensive nature of the Eskimo world-view is found expressed in the language, which is passive rather than active (Werkmeister 1939). In studies such as this, the world-view is revealed *independently* of the language analysis, and is then shown to be related. Reference to the language does not even confirm that a particular feature of mind is vital or at all noteworthy, for as we have seen, linguistic peculiarities may be semantically dead, the obsolete signs of some historical fact.

In conclusion, we can fully acknowledge the genetically fundamental role of language in the formation of the Lebenswelt, and we should note the occasional usefulness to the sociologist of semantic-linguistics as a potentially suggestive line of approach to the Lebenswelt. For other purposes, a thorough analysis of the constitution of the Lebenswelt would be intimately bound up with the phenomenology of language. For a verstehende sociology, an understanding of the subject's language is itself a prerequisite, since this is an intrinsic part of his behaviour and his life. But as far as the primary nature of language in relation to thought and perception is concerned, this is no essential part of sociology, even of phenomenological sociology, whose object is to penetrate and reveal the meanings and the general world-view of a social consciousness and, going beyond that, of a social group.

iii Knowledge and interest—ideology

At the beginning of this chapter, I criticised Marxist and other theories of ideology and knowledge for a certain crudity and superficiality in their conception of the determining co-ordinates of ideologically distorted and socially/materially based knowledge. This judgment must now, in a sense, be reversed. My point was that analysis on the macro-sociological level takes too many things for granted. The argument that material conditions, social relations and any other contingent factors are able to determine the superstructure of thought and ideation pre-supposes, but does not elucidate, a theory of the constitution of knowledge. It does not, it is true, necessarily assume a basic philosophical phenomenalism (the theory that we *cannot* know 'reality' as such, but only the world as mediated by our senses), or a fundamental relativity, nor does it condemn naïve realism. Such sociological theories of knowledge are entirely consistent with realism and objectivism. Nevertheless, the possibility of the social-experiential determination of the view of the world, from values to cognition itself, is implicit in these theories. I have argued that only the philosophical analysis of mind can reveal the basis for the justification of such theories. There would be no reason otherwise to believe, for example, that perception and belief were even *capable* of distortion beyond certain (in this case, irrelevant) limits, such as physical disorders of the senses, illogical or unscientific theorising, although this argument, of course, clearly only applies in areas of *cognitive* experience. I hope that the two preceding sections of this chapter go some way towards elucidating the way in which the mind and its modes of thought are social, linguistic and experiential creations. On this basis, the value of the discoveries of the traditional sociologists of knowledge must be appreciated.

I do not propose to review the classical theories of Marx and post-Marxian writers on this subject, much less to criticise them in their finer detail, but merely to recapitulate the basic argument common to them all, with reference to one or two authors. The more fundamental philosophical psychology of the earlier sections of this chapter must be expanded into, and supplemented by, the socio-political understanding of some of the most important determinants of ideology. This is all the more true today, when the limits of the scientific method, even in the natural sciences, are recognised, and the guarantee and possibility of objective, impartial knowledge are in question. The essential need for self-consciousness and reflection in this atmosphere of ubiquitous ideology has already been stressed by several writers (cf. Gouldner 1971; Habermas 1970, 1971a and b, 1972). The manner in which social factors influence thought, including sociological theory, must at least be exposed and thus, to some extent, controlled, if it cannot be eradicated.

The philosophy of mind and the philosophy of language have shown the essential perspectivism of thought, and suggested some of the ways in which the genetic process operates. (There are, indeed, others who argue for the existence of certain *innate* capacities and structuring forces of the mind, starting with the eighteenth-century rationalist philosophers and the Kantian categories, and including, among contemporary writers, particularly Chomsky, in the field of linguistics, Lévi-Strauss in anthropology, and Piaget in psychology.

33

This is not the place to dispute the possibility of, or at least the possibility of the *knowledge* of, such innate mental equipment; in another context, Lévi-Strauss's version will be referred to below. Although I am exceedingly sceptical of the validity of demonstrating these features of mind, the theories in question do not necessarily conflict with our basic tenet here, which is that, to a greater or lesser extent, ways of thinking and experiencing are both defined and limited by language and socialisation.) The sociological tradition deriving from Marx, similarly concerned with the social influences on knowledge and thought, investigates the ideological distortions and definitions of reality imposed by the dominant social group. This too is entirely consonant with the approaches which have just been considered. Its originality lies in its recognition that, given that world-views are in the simplest sense *arbitrary*, the actual 'choice' of world-view is closely linked with *interest* and *function*. In Marx's case, the interest was that of the ruling class, imposing (though perhaps with the same false consciousness of its authenticity as the oppressed class) its own view of the world. The motivating interests are basically those of social relations (power and authority), themselves founded on the economic-technological relations of production in society. Mannheim, maintaining the fundamental Marxist view of class as a basic determinant of knowledge, recognised the added complexities of modern technological societies, and thought that generation, for example, was another important substructural component in material life. Weber's classic studies in the sociology of religion, particularly *The Protestant ethic and the spirit of capitalism*, serve as a warning against a one-sided view of the relationship between economy and ideology. He has shown, and others have since confirmed, that religion and other ideological, or superstructural, factors can in their turn play an important determining role in economic motivation and behaviour. But the consensus among all these writers, and others who have appended their own particular modifications to the Marxian–Mannheimian sociology of knowledge, is that knowledge is closely related to interest.

There are two provisos to be made here. The first is that it is not always agreed what 'knowledge' refers to. Clearly, there are areas of thought which are without doubt ideological—values, religion, political ideology, for example. But it is not always obvious whether language, art and philosophy are claimed to be subject to the same relativistic determinism, much less the so-called objective areas of knowledge of perception, cognition and science. Second, the *nature* of the relationship between material base and knowledge is rarely specified; this could be one of straightforward causal determination, of reflection, of functional integration, or simply of consonance. We might add the final complicating comment that as ideology, founded as it is in social life, in its turn may have an effect *on* social institutions, in a dialectic of interdependence (just as language, which directs and limits experience in the ways we have seen, is itself an artefact of earlier social interaction), it becomes impossible to perceive how one could begin to develop a formula for the sociological constitution of knowledge. The dialectic, indeed, is confronted and explicated by Berger and Luckmann, and Marxist theory in general, so long as it retains its Hegelian dialectical heritage, is capable at least of conceiving the mutual interdependence of the dual aspects; but static, synchronic analysis is forced to adopt an arbitrary standpoint, and to take as given a large section of social life, ignoring its genetic features.

One of the most recent theories of knowledge in the Marxian tradition is found in the work of Jurgen Habermas. I shall be discussing Habermas again in a later chapter, in connection with hermeneutic philosophy and its critique. The particular relevance of his sociology of knowledge in this context is that it develops the Marxist analysis, refines it, and at the same time is explicitly aware of the phenomenological-linguistic constitution of knowledge. His thesis is that knowledge is determined by the three constitutive interests arising in work, language, and authority (Habermas 1966). In his constant primary concern with the methodology of the social sciences, he reaches this view through a historico-analytical critique of the methodological schools of sociology and history (Habermas 1970 and 1972). Thus, positivism and the empirical–analytical sciences are linked with the cognitive interest in *technical control* over objectified processes; the historical–hermeneutic sciences, with their understanding of meaning and expression, are linked with the *practical* cognitive interest ('a constitutive interest in the preservation and expansion of the inter-subjectivity of possible action-orienting mutual understanding . . . directed . . . toward the attainment of possible consensus among actors'—1972, Appendix, p. 310); critical social science is linked with an *emancipatory* cognitive interest, and here alone is methodology re-united with philosophy, from which positivism initiated a progressive process of divergence. The only valid methodology is a simultaneous act of *self*-reflection, and thus emancipation from authority. It is worth quoting Habermas at greater length here (1972, Appendix, p. 313):

The specific viewpoints from which, with transcendental necessity, we apprehend reality ground three categories of possible knowledge: information that expands our power of technical control; interpretations that make possible the orientation of action within common traditions; and analyses that free consciousness from its dependence on hypostatized powers. These viewpoints originate in the interest structure of a species that is linked in its roots to definite means of social organization: work, language, and power. The human species secures its existence in systems of social labor and self-assertion through violence, through tradition-bound social life in ordinary-language communication, and with the aid of ego identities that at every level of individuation reconsolidate the consciousness of the individual in relation to the norms of the group. Accordingly the interests constitutive of knowledge are linked to the functions of an ego that adapts itself to its external conditions through learning processes, is initiated into the communication system of a social life-world by means of self-formative processes, and constructs an identity in the conflict between instinctual aims and social constraints. In turn these achievements become part of the productive forces accumulated by a society, the cultural tradition through which a society interprets itself, and the legitimations that a society accepts or criticizes. . . . Knowledge-constitutive interests take form in the medium of work, language, and power.

In his specifically directed criticisms of Gadamer (Habermas 1971a and b), Habermas further develops the conception of sociology as ideology-critique, which, incorporating the linguistic and hermeneutic revisions of positivism, goes further (or, one might say, back) into an objective (that is, self-reflective) extra-phenomenological perspective. In this way, as Habermas remarks (1972, p. 197), the possibility is re-opened of 'pursuing methodology in the *epistemological mode*', which is 'the experience of the emancipatory power of reflection, which the subject experiences in itself to the extent that it becomes transparent to itself in the history of its genesis'. But in *Zur Logik der Sozialwissenschaften* (1970) it is clear that his ideology-critique is founded on those theories of knowledge which he nevertheless finds it necessary to attack for their limitations. It is for this reason that he says (1972, Preface, p. xii) 'a radical critique of knowledge is possible only as social theory'. The following passage, in the context of his critique of scientific positivism, illustrates the congruence of Habermas's sociology of knowledge with that which is being proposed here (1972, pp. 68–9):

The positivistic attitude conceals the problem of world constitution. *The meaning of knowledge itself becomes irrational* —in the name of rigorous knowledge. In this way, the naïve idea that knowledge describes reality becomes prevalent. This is accompanied by the copy theory of truth, according to which the reversibly univocal correlation of statements and matters of fact must be understood as isomorphism . . . The illusion of objectivism can no longer be dispelled by a return to Kant but only immanently—by forcing methodology to carry out a process of self-reflection in terms of its own problems. Objectivism deludes the sciences with the image of a self-subsistent world of facts structured in a lawlike manner; it thus conceals the a priori constitution of these facts.

The importance of Habermas's insistence on the epistemological revision of sociological methodology, amounting as it does to a methodology rooted in and inseparable from a sociology of knowledge, is that it achieves the unique synthesis of two essential and formerly disparate critiques of knowledge: the micro-analysis of the individual, phenomenological-linguistic experience, and the macro- or social analysis of knowledge-constitutive determining interests.

3   The problems of the sociology of knowledge

There are two fundamental interests underlying this essay, which are analytically distinct but at the same time, I would maintain, interdependent. The first, which has been examined in the preceding chapter, is the epistemological question of the nature of knowledge and its experiential, social, linguistic, material and ideological determinants. The second is the methodological question of the nature and theory of sociological understanding (discussed in part in chapter 1). The sociology of knowledge is, or should be, their natural meeting point, and yet they have nearly always been strictly separated by academic discipline boundaries, the first in particular being considered philosophy and thus not relevant to sociology. The phenomenological analysis of the *social* construction of reality which we have been investigating helps to bridge the gap, at least from one end, by showing that sociology is certainly relevant to epistemological questions of knowledge-constitution. But it is equally important to recognise that the second question also involves the first: that is, that sociological theory itself must incorporate an awareness of the grounds of knowledge—in this case, sociological knowledge. The sociology of sociology, as part of the sociology of knowledge, is also part of the theory and method of sociology. Thus, my attempt to fuse these two interests is not an arbitrary whim, but seems to me to be the essential prerequisite both for the satisfactory resolution of each question, and for the sociology of knowledge.

The analyses of the preceding two chapters and the recognition of the social and experiential determinants of knowledge in addition serve to reformulate the traditional paradoxes of the sociology of knowledge. In particular, the essential relativity of the sociologist's own statements and observations appears unavoidable, and the question of the objectivity of the social sciences is forced upon us for re-appraisal, in the light of the phenomenological understanding of knowledge-constitution. (In a later chapter, the hermeneutic resolution of both these problems will be discussed, when Gadamer's potential contribution to the sociology of knowledge is considered.) Furthermore, the relationship between epistemology and ontology also becomes clear, for a theory of inevitable perspectivism raises the question of a 'real' world and revives the philosophical debates of nominalism versus realism, and phenomenalism versus Platonic idealism. The three major issues of relativity, objectivity and reality are, it is my argument, inseparable. When this is seen, it must also be accepted, not only that sociological theory, the sociology of knowledge, epistemology and ontology are interconnected, but, more radically, that sociological theory itself necessarily involves these other theories of knowledge and reality. In this chapter, I want to look more closely at some of the philosophical problems of the sociology of knowledge and of sociological theory. Having argued that epistemology involves ontology, I shall nevertheless leave ontological problems to one side for the moment, and concentrate here on theories of knowledge.

i Relativity and the problem of objective knowledge

The circularity of the sociology of knowledge has been recognised for a long time. Mannheim attempted to provide an answer by positing the 'free-floating intelligentsia' as furthest removed from existential-ideological distortion, achieving objective thought through their acquaintance with more than one possible perspective. Marxist theories impute the possibility of non-perspectivist knowledge to the proletariat, once it can rid itself of its false consciousness. Merton's comment on such epistemological defences is also well-known. 'These efforts to rescue oneself from an extreme relativism parallel Munchhausen's feat of extricating himself from a swamp by pulling on his whiskers' (Merton 1957, p. 507). His own recommendation is that sociological questions of knowledge be kept distinct from 'epistemological impedimenta' (p. 508). Bottomore (1956) has also argued that the problem is only apparent, and arises from the mistaken confusion of two kinds of question (p. 55).

The theory of ideology is, no doubt, as important in sociology as is the theory of 'rationalization' in psychology. It is also prone to the same excesses when it claims either to resolve, or to eliminate, epistemological problems. I do not question the interest and value of the studies of ideology which Marx and Mannheim, and later sociologists, have made. My criticisms are intended to show the limitations of this analysis of ideologies, and to indicate its place in a more general sociology of knowledge.

39

He concludes (p. 57):

> The kind of study I am recommending would aim simply
> at describing and analysing some of the more important
> ways in which knowledge is conserved, extended, suppressed
> or revived, in different societies and at different times. For
> whatever our philosophic doubts about knowledge and
> knowing, we cannot be doubtful about the occurrence of a
> social selection of ideas; and this is a matter of the greatest
> sociological interest.

For both these sociologists, the epistemological issue does not arise, since it is defined as outside the scope of the *sociological* analysis of knowledge.

Max Weber, in his methodological writings, also concludes that the social position of the sociologist himself, and the value-relevance of his researches, in no way damages the scientific nature of the enquiry and the objectivity of the results. (See especially 'Politics as a vocation' and 'Science as a vocation', Weber 1947a; and Weber 1968.) The sociologist has the duty to keep apart his dual roles of social scientist and political-social being. 'The investigator and teacher should keep unconditionally separate the establishment of empirical facts (including the "value-oriented" conduct of the empirical individual whom he is investigating) and *his* own practical evaluations' (1968, p. 11). Values only come into the initial stages of sociological enquiry, in the selection of problems of investigation, but Weber insists that the value-freedom of the enquiry itself is a different matter, which by following the canons of scientific method and causal, ideal-typical analysis, can continue to be guaranteed within these limits. (Gadamer, as I shall show in a later chapter, rejected this dissociation of value-relevance from the value-freedom, or objectivity, of the investigation, arguing that the prejudices of the social scientist or cultural historian are an intrinsic part of his enquiry, and, furthermore, that only through them can a kind of objectivity be achieved.) Thus, although Weber recognises the fact that man is, even if he is a social scientist, also a social and political being, he never doubts that we need only to rely on method to eliminate entirely any possible problem of perspectivism. It is important to notice that Weber, like the other sociologists just mentioned, is far from being a strict positivist, in whom one might expect such confidence in the potential of the scientific method. The point is that a sociologist who advocates the use of Verstehen and who recognises the relevance of subjective factors, motives and intentions, to the data of sociological observation, at the same time feels able to support his method against charges of unscientific procedure and lack of objectivity.

Earlier I argued that the phenomenological school of sociology can be seen as a continuation of the Weberian tradition of verstehende sociology (p. 5 above). The phenomenologists, however, recognise the implications of their method for the scientific status of the discipline (J. Douglas 1971, p. 25).

Once we recognize that all knowledge, certainly all knowledge of meaningful human phenomena, is ultimately grounded in our common-sense experience and, therefore, can never be totally examined and purged of 'unrationalized' or practical elements and relations, then we must conclude that the foundation of all classical science, the *absolutist conception of objectivity*, can never be achieved.

This is so because a proper analysis of the understanding achieved by the sociologist makes clear the part played in the process by his own existential situation. It does not, according to Douglas, lead to the collapse of sociological method or the impossibility of any research (p. 26).

To recognize the necessity of rejecting classical objectivity does not mean that we must or should relinquish our search for objective knowledge. It simply means that we must modify our theory of knowledge and our conception of objectivity.

The antidote to relativism of thought is achieved by progressively freeing the knowledge of the facts from the situation in which they are known, for example by examining the research methods employed (pp. 29–30), although, as Douglas adds, 'presumably there will always remain that irreducible dependence on common-sense understandings of everyday life' (p. 31). 'Objective' knowledge is now seen as 'trans-situational' knowledge, attained by 'further "reductions", or deeper analyses, of everyday life' (p. 35). The same conclusion is reached by Peter McHugh (1971), on analysing the failure of positivism. 'We needn't abandon the idea of objectivity so long as we recognize that objectivity is made possible by having met a *generally accepted rule of procedure* within the collectivity' ('On the failure of positivism', in Douglas 1971, p. 333). McHugh's enquiry arises not only from the problem of the circularity of the sociology of knowledge but, more fundamentally, from the philosophical analysis of knowledge itself, and the recognition that 'there is no tenable epistemology for a single world of real objects' (p. 334). His radical summary is that (p. 335):

It is necessary to remove the province of truth from the physical object world to the social world. No canon, no collective, no institution can go outside itself to a world of independent objects for criteria of knowledge, since there is no other way except by its own rules to describe what's being done with regard to knowledge. . . . Sociological truth, as with any other kind, exists only because sociology has generated its own ways of conceding truth. It is not an aggregation of private people sensing individual objects, but a public, rule-guided, and institutionalized canon of social procedure.

Such a total relativisation of knowledge and of truth itself is, I feel, too extreme. Just as I would challenge Bottomore's and Merton's rather facile dismissal of all epistemological debate from the socio-logical field, so I would object to the radical phenomenologists' and ethnomethodologists' over-confident takeover and absorption into sociology of what are, in the end, still philosophical questions. Furthermore it is important not to confuse here two separate problems. The first is the extent to which, and the way in which, the sociologist's researches are coloured and distorted by his own social-existential position. The second is the epistemological question of the sense in which one can speak of the real, or objective, world, and whether such a world is knowable. McHugh's position depends on the premiss that the answer to the second question is negative, and this determines his way of dealing with the first. But Bottomore refuses to consider the second question, and reserves the sociologist's energies for the first. Weber, I am inclined to suggest, implicitly answers the epistemological question in the affirmative (with respec-tably neo-Kantian refinements), and directs his attention to the task of demonstrating how the sociologist can best approximate to such objective knowledge. I have said that the philosophy of knowledge and the sociology of knowledge necessarily intersect at many points, and I am not, by differentiating two analytically distinct issues, retracting my statement here. The solution to the theoretical problem of relativity of knowledge must, in a sense, fall somewhere between the extremes of the sociological purism of Bottomore and the radical relativism of some phenomenologists. It must be prepared to deal with the epistemological issues involved in the social creation of knowledge, without simply defining epistemology out of existence or relegating it to a sub-branch of sociology in the process. The following statement by Gurvitch summarises the argument accurately (1971, p. 11):

If collaboration, negative as well as positive, is established between the sociology of knowledge and philosophy, the domination of one over the other is excluded. To deduce an epistemology from the sociology of knowledge would be as illfated as to link the fate of the sociology of knowledge to a particular philosophical position. Besides, from all points of view, it is essential for the development of the sociology of knowledge that it learn to remain modest and renounce inordinate pretensions.

And (p. 19):

It is therefore a question of joint collaboration between the sociology of knowledge and epistemology which, though remaining irreducible, render mutual service.

ii Knowledge and reality

Knowledge of the world has long been at the centre of philosophical concerns and had been debated for centuries before sociology also came to self-consciousness and began to see it as problematic. Philosophical theories of knowledge remain for the most part oblivious of the parallel sociological arguments, and may be considered briefly here as the more fundamental discussion in terms of which sociological relativity and the question of objective knowledge in the social sciences make sense. A sound epistemological understanding, even one ignorant of the sociology of knowledge, is essential if one is to avoid the excesses of total relativism in this area, or the epistemological sociologism of McHugh.

The classical conception of a Real (or Ideal) world to which we have access, both made possible and at the same time limited by our perceptual and mental apparatus and our situational circumstances, has long been abandoned by the mainstream of modern European philosophy (which is usually dated from Descartes in France and Locke in England). The empiricists' analyses led to the conclusion that the only world we *know* is the world of sense data; Berkeley's phenomenalism demonstrates that we cannot know that the tree in the yard is still there when we are not perceiving it (and goes on to rescue the world from this precarious existence by pointing out that as God is always perceiving the tree, as well as everything else, there *is* a continuing world of objects). More recent sense-data theory, without relying on theological argument, has also concluded that the material world we experience is merely the sum of our sense-data of it, and that we cannot talk of any ultimate reality. In the Continental rationalist tradition, phenomenology follows the insights of Descartes, who reduced absolute knowledge to the Cogito (i.e., although I can be deceived by misperception, hallucination, false memory, and many other things in my knowledge, I can at least be certain of the fact that I, at this very moment, think). Descartes, too, attempted to rebuild the world by virtue of his faith in God, who, being infinitely good, would not work systematically to deceive us in our perceptions and experiences. Modern phenomenology is aware that indeed we *cannot* go beyond the Cogito, and that in a sense the objective, scientific world of material objects is lost forever. Husserl argues that the only way to re-establish the world, without any leap of faith and without deviating from the standard of the only sure knowledge of the Cogito, is to 'bracket' both the natural attitude to the world and the scientific attitude (the phenomenological 'epoché') and to constitute the world through the phenomena of consciousness. One could perhaps rephrase this by saying that, as doubts can be raised with regard to the foundation and certainty of all our knowledge and beliefs except that we *have* these beliefs and experiences, then we must restrict our talk of the outside world to the world-as-experienced. Husserl felt that a new science, more sound epistemologically than the existing sciences, simply because it does not start with any axiomatic assumptions of a world taken for granted, could be built within this phenomenological method.

In general then, the idea of an objectively existing world, apart from our experience of it, is discredited on all sides. At best one can take the Kantian position that if there is such a world, which is beyond the phenomena and which is the origin of these, we can neither know it nor say anything about it. This concept of a noumenal reality is, of course, rather strange, for one might wonder how such a reality can even be mentioned in this context: does it, in fact, make sense to say 'there is a reality which we cannot know or talk about', and if so, how can we *know* that there is? Scheler's theory of knowledge is equally suspect, for he actually posits the existence of an ideal (i.e. objectively existing) world, to which our actual situation gives us limited access (Scheler 1926). Since arguments in the sociology of knowledge are also of this kind, it is important to clarify what is meant by the ultimately real world, which is often implicit in theories of knowledge. It is also important to distinguish the *different* ways in which this same phrase might be used, for the failure to do this has resulted in much of the epistemological confusion on the subject. To begin with, given that, as we have seen, social and other factors and interests may distort one's interpretation and perception of the world, then it is clear that in one sense at least it is legitimate to talk about an objective world, or of eliminating distortion in perspective. Even here, 'the world' includes both the basic material world (chairs, people, natural or man-made objects, physical events, like avalanches), and the social-cultural world of symbolic behaviour, institutions, roles, conventions. In the case of the latter, perhaps, it is questionable whether there *could* be non-interpretative (and thus objective) observation of the world, although it remains true that ideological distortion can be corrected to an extent or counterbalanced by an opposing perspective. But philosophical theories of knowledge, unlike their sociological counterparts, are concerned primarily with the material world, and even here the separate levels of 'reality' are to be distinguished (see section (iv) below).

The concept of a 'real world' seems paradoxical. On the one hand, it can be shown that our view of the world (including the world of material objects) is determined and directed by our language, our learned ways of perceiving, our social situation and interests, and that, in some respects at least, not only can such filters not be eliminated, but they are the essential prerequisites *for* experience. Gestalt psychology and existential-phenomenological philosophy demonstrate that experience of the world is necessarily interpretative, with the corollary that any experience outside a life-world of meaning cannot itself be meaningful or properly grasped. On the other hand, if recognition of this perspectivism implies the existence of an ideal world, on which one has some perspective or other, it is difficult to see how this world may be discovered, discussed or even conceived. It may well be that the paradox arises from linguistic abuse, and from the confusion of the various meanings of 'reality' and 'objectivity'.

iii Cross-cultural understanding

The problem of objective observation and research is compounded when cross-cultural investigation is considered. The anthropologist, sociologist or historian is confronted, in the light of the preceding critique of knowledge, with a dual challenge. There is the task of eliminating, or at least incorporating an explicit recognition of, his own socially bound perspective in his theorising and observations. There is also the task of finding some way of dealing with the culture under study; assuming that one wants to approach it in its own terms, as perceived and interpreted by its members, the problem then becomes one of deciding what would be the objectively existing culture, purified of both the social scientist's and the native inhabitant's prejudices. If, as seems likely, the idea of a non-interpretative understanding is inconceivable as far as certain aspects of knowledge are concerned, then it rather looks as though objectivity in cross-cultural research is an impossible aim.

Nineteenth-century historicist theories provide an attempt to overcome the dilemma of historical knowledge. In particular, the writings of Dilthey propose this theory; Collingwood in England later put forward similar ideas (Collingwood 1961). The primary insistence of historicism is that the past must be considered in its own language and in terms of its own contemporary self-image; it should not be approached through the arbitrary interpreting schemata imposed by the historian's own frame of reference, placed firmly in the present. The historian, according to Dilthey, must attempt to perform the empathic act of transporting himself into the past, and thus becoming part of the culture he is studying, at the same time eliminating his present ego and transcending the contemporary factors influencing his experience, his view of the world and, particularly, his research. The notion of empathic understanding of a culture is one taken over by Weber in his concept of Verstehen, as intrinsic to the sociological method, although his objections to Dilthey's unscientific account led him to formulate in careful detail the subsequent procedures of a truly scientific method, which could also incorporate subjective understanding. But without considering Weber's criticisms or the place of causal explanation, ideal types, and empirical verification in the social sciences (for these questions of method in fact do little to clarify the fundamental issue of cross-cultural understanding), the historicist argument is suspect. There is no reason to believe that the total annihilation of the self is a possibility; it seems highly unlikely that the historian, or the sociologist, could ever come to his material with an entirely open mind in this sense. In a later chapter, I shall discuss Gadamer's revision of this oversimplified historicism, and suggest that his account of cross-cultural investigation as a 'blending of horizons' of past and present, or of one society and another, is far more convincing.

iv The levels and varieties of knowledge

Both the philosophical and the sociological theories of knowledge must be aware of the danger of using 'knowledge' as a vaguely general term without defining its exact reference in a particular context. Here one or two suggestions will merely be put forward concerning some analytical distinctions which can be made within the category, in the belief that such clarification is the first step in the attempt to comprehend the conditions and determinants of knowledge, and to examine methodically the possibilities of non-perspectivist, objective knowledge.

At the higher, or more complex, level of knowledge-of-the-world is what Mannheim called 'particular ideology'. This is ideology in its usual sense of political or social beliefs and values. The implication is that an avoidable distortion is involved, and furthermore, as the distortion is in accordance with the person's interests, this conception of ideology has a derogatory connotation. It is concerned only with specific aspects of the world, and in this it differs from the 'total' ideology of a person or group. To quote Mannheim on the concept of a particular ideology (1966, p. 49):

> The particular conception of ideology is implied when the
> term denotes that we are sceptical of the ideas and representations
> advanced by our opponent. They are regarded as more or less

conscious disguises of the real nature of a situation, the true recognition of which would not be in accord with his interest.

(Note that Mannheim, in his use of the phrase 'the *true* recognition of which' clearly considers particular ideologies to be eliminable.) The total ideology, in Mannheim's terms is 'the ideology of an age or of a concrete historico-social group, e.g. of a class, when we are concerned with the characteristics and composition of the total structure of the mind of this epoch or of this group' (pp. 49–50). Both kinds of ideology are seen as functions of the person who holds them, or of his social position. They are contrasted in their scope (total ideology being the whole Weltanschauung, 'including his conceptual apparatus', of the individual), their level (particular ideology operating purely on the psychological level, and total ideology on the theoretical or noological level), and their subject-matter (the psychology of interests and motives as against the structural differences of mind). Clearly the total ideology, or world-view, of the individual, is of a more fundamental nature than the particular, and is, indeed, its sub-structure. Mannheim argues that, unlike particular ideologies, total ideologies are necessary conditions of thought. 'The vain hope of discovering truth in a form which is independent of an historically and socially determined set of meanings will have to be given up' (op. cit. p. 71). Whereas a psychological study of interests is sufficient to expose and discredit particular ideologies and produce non-ideological (on this level) thought, the sociology of knowledge is not able to do more than demonstrate the ideological (in the total sense) nature of knowledge. As Mannheim puts it: 'The question then arises: which social standpoint vis-à-vis of history offers the best chance for reaching an optimum of truth?' (ibid.). And truth itself, it appears, is not an absolute conception of a reality, grasped in limited form by the world-views of human existence (pp. 94–5).

> Totality in the sense in which we conceive it is not an immediate and eternally valid vision of reality attributable only to a divine eye. It is not a self-contained and stable view. On the contrary, a total view implies both the assimilation and transcendance of the limitations of particular points of view. It represents the continuous process of the expansion of knowledge, and has as its goal not achievement of a super-temporally valid conclusion but the broadest possible extension of our horizon of vision.

(It is interesting, too, to compare this conception of truth with Gadamer's ontology, which it prefigures in certain respects. See chapter 7 below.)

The particular and total conceptions of ideology give us an

47

important distinction between two types of knowledge-of-the-world. Nevertheless, Mannheim uses total ideology to cover a number of levels in itself. For example, the 'conceptual apparatus' he includes seems to me to be a more fundamental aspect of knowledge than the ideology of class interests. Within total ideology, or world-view, we may distinguish first (and closest to particular ideology) views of society, of social institutions and of one's own position in the social structure. (I am not here moving from talking about levels or types of knowledge to talking of the content or subject-matter of knowledge, except inasmuch as perspectivism of thought differs precisely *in* such different areas of knowledge.) Here we may suppose that values and interests play a relatively large part in ideological perspective, and that socialisation and social and cultural background are paramount factors in the interpretative process. Next one might put the less specific, more diffuse, Weltanschauung of the general cosmology (religious, quasi-religious, totemic, mythological, etc.); beliefs about society are seen as an extension or off-shoot of this general cosmology. (Durkheim, however, reverses this interpretation, considering the categories of all experience of the world to be social in origin.) Again, socialisation, including language-learning, is relevant to the acquisition and maintenance of world-view on this level, although interests and values may be thought to be less directly involved. More basic still is simple experience of the material world—the traditional area of enquiry of epistemology. (Existential analysis and Gestalt psychology, however, import even into this level some of the complexities of the 'higher' forms of knowledge. Their premiss is that *any* experience is interpreted within the total world of experience of the individual and thus, presumably, the simple perception of a table, for example, itself is bound up with other, more complex, aspects of world-view, values and view of society.) One can differentiate too within this fundamental level of experience and knowledge, more or less interpretative, or culturally-linked, perceptions. For example, the action of a man felling a tree is less open to symbolic interpretation within a system of meanings than, say, a man handing money to another man (although, of course, a knowledge of why trees are felled and to what use—practical, magical, etc.—they are put, is also essential in the first case). On the other hand, to understand the interpretation by a society of a tree being struck by lightning, the general frame of reference of their cosmology, scientific ideas and religious beliefs must first be grasped.

The object of this section has been to point out that an undifferentiated concept of 'knowledge' is a serious hindrance to the philosophical and sociological analyses of knowledge. There will continue to be confused argument as to whether knowledge can be 'objective' and 'non-relative' as long as the *kind* of knowledge at issue remains unclarified. On the subject of the different forms of knowledge, we might mention here Parsons's threefold distinction of cognitive, effective and evaluative knowledge (Parsons 1951). This categorisation is also extremely suggestive as an orientation in the examination of the various modes and extents of ideological distortion in knowledge. Gurvitch (1971) has also given much thought to the question of the varieties of knowledge (p. 14).

> Even the most dogmatic sociologists and philosophers distinguish two or even three types of knowledge—philosophical knowledge, scientific knowledge, and technical knowledge. For our part, we consider that there exists a much larger number of types of knowledge, which the sociology of knowledge, as well as epistemology must take into consideration, and each of these types acts as a frame of reference, thus eliminating the dogma of the universal validity of judgments.

His own classification of the types of knowledge might well be taken as a starting point for the type of analysis recommended in this section.

v Structure and the individual

The structure-versus-individual debate recurs in a variety of contexts, and is relevant, too, to the sociology of knowledge.

a The ontological debate, usually in terms of holism versus individualism, concerns the possibility of talking of society as an entity of any kind, apart from the individuals who compose it. Durkheim's conception of society as a reality *sui generis* has been challenged on philosophical grounds, in the same way as the Hegelian view of history is attacked for a false metaphysics of being. Conciliation is often achieved by allowing the concept of 'society' as an heuristic term. More sophisticated (and, I would maintain, correct) dialectical accounts acknowledge the 'real' existence of society, though not, of course, as a material object, or as 'real' in the same sense as a person is real, while recognising at the same time its origin in individuals and their past and present interactions (see Berger and Luckmann 1967).

b Ethics and political philosophy pursue a similar argument. Here the debate is whether obligation is to the state (some versions of social contract theory, as well as political Hegelianism) or to individuals (utilitarianism).

c In the context of methodology, and related to the ontological issue (a), the question of legitimate units of analysis arises. The two sides are epitomised by the contemporary, and diametrically opposed, schools of structural-functionalism and structuralism, and

49

phenomenological sociology and ethnomethodology. The former includes Lévi-Strauss in anthropology and Parsonian theory in sociology; the latter includes Schutz, Berger and Luckmann, and a number of more recent writers. As I shall point out later (chapter 5 (i)), Ricoeur advocates an attempt to merge the two standpoints in a structuralism which is also sensitive to individual meanings. The decision as to whether one takes the social structure or the social individual as one's frame of reference is in a sense merely a question of choice, and the decision may depend, for example, on the explanatory potential of either model in sociological enquiry.

d The issue nevertheless becomes a debate about values and politics, when phenomenologists maintain that structuralism (or at least structural-functionalism) is inherently conservative, taking as it does the *status quo* as its starting-point. This particular criticism, to be fair, is more usually made by radical sociologists and Marxist conflict theorists (who are equally opposed to 'liberal' phenomenology). However, the case of deviancy theory is an excellent example of a situation where values invade analysis. In structural terms, deviance is inevitably seen as deviance *from* the system (although its functions as well as its dysfunctions can be recognised). Thus from the point of view of the structuralist-sociologist, the deviant is on the whole a problem, and the major interest is in ways of dealing with him, or incorporating him into the social structure (Merton 1957, chapter IV). Starting from the point of view *of* the deviant, in contrast, phenomenological-existential sociology comprehends his behaviour in terms of its meaning for him, and his own motives, in the world of his experience (including, of course, his own position in society, and his own view of society) (Cohen 1971). Here it is clear that political values determine methodology. It might, and most probably does, also mean that structural-functionalists are in general conservative in politics, and that phenomenologists are liberal or even radical. But it does *not* necessarily mean that their researches are themselves value-laden. This is a mistake which is made on both sides. At most one can say that structural sociology can be used politically in a conservative way, but not constructively in a progressive way, and vice versa, for various forms of radical sociology. But both forms of sociological analysis can be accurate and objective, providing a contribution to knowledge, albeit from different standpoints and within different world-views.

e Still on the question of methodology, one might take the straightforwardly evaluative position that structural analysis is immoral, being essentially anti-humanist and not giving primary importance to the dignity of the individual. This is not a position which can be proved, or even defended, by argument; neither can it be supported, as might the similarly arbitrary choice of phenomenology as a method, by demonstrating that it has better explanatory value than its alternatives. I mention it merely because I hold it.[1]

f   The sociology of knowledge involves a certain commitment on this question, and raises questions of its own in the same area. Despite the fact that only an individual or individuals can 'know', structural analysis is also possible in the field of knowledge. Marxist analyses of the superstructure are one example; even Mannheim's essay on generations (Mannheim 1968) is at the level of society and of the knowledge of the social group. (In the following section and in chapter 4, I shall consider certain important objections to this supra-individual concept of 'knowledge'.) In one way, the sociology of knowledge is able to reconcile the two perspectives, inasmuch as it attempts to show how the individual's view of the world is a product (in the ways discussed earlier) of his society—its language, institutions, values and conventions. The major problem for the sociology of knowledge, in this particular context, is to find a way of mediating between the existential reality of the social individual and the societal structural aspects of his consciousness. Purely structural approaches are bound to work with an epistemologically and conceptually inadequate notion of 'knowledge' (see chapters 5 and 6 below). The phenomenological perspective, on the other hand, which is in a better position to begin with the analysis of the constitution of knowledge in the individual consciousness, should also be able to accommodate the social and structural factors involved in the process of the acquisition of knowledge (at every level).

vi   The concept of a world-view

This question is discussed in detail in chapter 4. It is closely related to the debate, just referred to, between structure and the individual as theoretical perspectives. Where the structural point of view has the advantage here of being able to refer directly to the 'knowledge' of a society or a supra-individual group, the approach we are recommending must solve the problem of the meaning, sense and reference of the world-view of a *society*, as opposed to that of a social actor.

vii   Epistemology and ontology

Finally, we may return to the philosophical and metaphysical aspects of the sociology of knowledge. On the basis of the points made in some of the preceding sections of this chapter, it is now apparent how theory and method, epistemology and ontology, are interconnected. In chapter 2, we considered some of the ways in which

[1] On this subject, see Caws's argument, discussed in chapter 5(i) below.

knowledge is constituted. In section (ii) of the present chapter, the implications of this non-absolutist conception of knowledge for the metaphysical theory of being and of the world were pointed out. The theory of knowledge, in the process of revealing the foundations of knowledge of the world, simultaneously raises the question of the world *apart* from our knowledge of it. Speculative (as opposed to analytical or descriptive) metaphysics solves the problem by taking the step into religious faith, poetry or non-rational belief, at the expense of abandoning the analytical attitude and the possibility of argument and proof. In their different ways, Plato, Berkeley, Heidegger and Scheler thus defend the ultimate reality of the world. (Gadamer, it will later be seen, also resorts in the end to a similarly speculative ontology—chapter 7.) Refusing to follow this course, all we can say is that we cannot know or even sensibly talk about any reality beyond our knowledge-of-reality. To be sure, we can, by a critique of knowledge, expose and in some cases adjust our ways of knowing and the actual determinants *of* our knowing. We can also arrive at a more 'objective' reality by corroboration, whether of one person's perceptions and interpretations with those of another, or of the data of one of the senses with those of another, or of memory (to identify, for example, hallucinations or mistakes). Nuclear physics or molecular biology can penetrate deeper and deeper into the nature of matter, and in this sense get closer to the 'reality' behind appearances. But, in the end, we are left with appearances; epistemology involves and defines the limits of ontology, and there can be no ontology outside the critical theory of knowledge. Epistemology, in its turn, is inseparable from the sociological critique of knowledge, although not exhausted by it. On this last point, I quote Mannheim once more, in a statement which sums up much of the concern of this book (1966, p. 70).

> Epistemology is as intimately enmeshed in the social process as is the totality of our thinking, and it will make progress to the extent that it can master the complications arising out of the changing structure of thought.

4 The sociology of art and the concept of a world-view

A sociology of art, as a branch of the sociology of knowledge, shares all the theoretical problems of the latter. Thus the discussion of the preceding chapter should be seen to be equally relevant to the sociology of art. As has already been suggested (chapter 1), additional problems, specific to art and literature, arise in this area. In this section, therefore, I shall indicate what I consider the major difficulties to be; that is, I shall consider a little more closely what precisely a sociological theory of the arts attempts to discover, how this differs from other (e.g. aesthetic, or psychological) theories of art, whether and how such analysis is possible, and how this relates to our earlier discussion, concerning both the phenomenological method in sociology in general, and the sociology of knowledge. The controversial notion of a collective consciousness, or a social world-view, is crucial in this particular context, and an outline of the objections to such a concept leads to a review, in the two subsequent chapters, of attempts by a number of writers to come to terms with it, and to operationalise an extraordinarily elusive idea. This, again, deflects the discussion from the sociology of art as such, to concentrate on a rather narrow, though critically related, aspect of it. I shall reconsider the sociology of art and literature, in the light of this and other analytical excursions and theoretical investigations pursued in these pages, in the final chapter, where, it is hoped, one or two positive suggestions may be made as to the direction a sociology of art might profitably take.

If the sociology of knowledge demonstrates the social origin of ideational activity and of the corpus of all knowledge, then we might suppose that art too, as one form of knowledge, is similarly related to social factors. The point might here be raised that art is an individual, private creation, at least in the majority of cases (painting a picture, writing, if not performing, a play, composing, if not playing, a quartet), and thus that it is psychology rather than sociology which is in a position to relate it to other, non-aesthetic facts. To attribute Shakespeare's plays to the society of his time and not simply to Shakespeare himself is to commit a sociologistic fallacy. There are two points to be made in reply. In the first place, the artist is himself a social individual; if his art does indeed express his personal ideas and values, these ideas and values are, as we have seen, largely created in the social context. Furthermore, it might fairly safely be hypothesised that only non-eccentric art finds a resonance and acceptance in its contemporary society, and only to the extent that it does will it take its place in the artistic tradition, whether as continuing or as reforming it. In this sense, the individual's creation is social in its content and meanings. Second, it is in any case certainly in order from the point of view of methodology to demonstrate a relationship between works of art and social structure, and to ignore the mediating factor of the actual creator. It is perfectly acceptable to explain the change in the nature of French painting before and after the Revolution of 1789 in terms of political events and social climate, without even referring to, say, Fragonard and Watteau on the one hand, David on the other, let alone their personal feelings and motives in painting their works. Nevertheless, this type of purely sociological explanation is lacking in certain dimensions, as I suggested earlier, in particular the aesthetic and phenomenological, or action-level, perspectives. Thus, my case for supporting a sociology of art which is not reduced to more psychological accounts, rests on the first point.

The psychological study of art is itself an extremely important field of enquiry, and I should make it clear too that I am by no means advocating that this should be subsumed under, or abandoned in favour of, the sociology of art. Results of the various investigations in this area may, indeed, be able to be conjoined with those of sociologists in an even more enlightening understanding of artistic creativity. (Gombrich's (1960) *Art and illusion* provides an excellent example of a case where a theory of the psychology of perception in art is related to social aspects of learning, and a sociological-psychological view of aesthetic experience propounded.) It should also be noted, perhaps, that other theories of art are similarly considered valid within their own terms of reference. Traditional non-sociological history of art, and the intrinsic study of change, development and innovation within a genre is not here being attacked; neither is pure aesthetic theory, or the philosophy of art. My argument is that (a) art is (amongst other things) a social creation, and (b) the sociological study of art ideally should satisfy certain criteria.

The two fundamental questions which must be answered by an adequate sociology of art and literature are: (i) *which* social ideas, values, beliefs, are expressed in art? and (ii) *how* are they thus expressed? The second question, in particular, is ignored by most sociologists, and it is here that, as I am arguing, sociology must take account of aesthetics. The first question leads directly into the problem of societal world-views. It is clearly impossible, within the limits of this book, to develop either a critique of sociological theories of the arts (some examples of which are referred to in chapter 1) or a theory of aesthetics, and my intention is simply to raise these two issues of orientation as central to the discipline. The answer to the question of how art expresses social and other meanings seems to me to be almost exclusively one which is intrinsic to the study of art itself. Thus, for example, the philosophy of symbolic forms (Cassirer and Suzanne Langer), semiology (Barthes), or pure aesthetic theories (formalism, subjectivism, art-as-expression) may be invoked in such an account. Where there is no such discussion, I would be inclined to argue that there is, nevertheless, an *implicit* theory of artistic expression, for otherwise the sociologist could have no directives in his approach to art. Innumerable possibilities of significant features are presented to him, including content, representative elements, technical aspects (colour or perspective in painting, complexities of scoring in music), simple statements about social life, where they occur, allegory, etc. He must obviously work with some preconception as to how he will analyse the works he is studying. But a theory which remains implicit also runs the risk of containing confusions and contradictions. For this reason it is felt that the sociological (and any other) study of art must include a formulated conception of the expressive qualities of art and the pertinent respects in which the arts may be said to express or reflect extra-artistic ideas. The case of the direct documentary content of a novel is only the simplest, most straightforward, example of how meanings in an art-form may be related to other facts of social life.

The problem of *what*, outside itself, art expresses is, on the other hand, one for the sociologist and not the aesthetician. It is the analyst of social life and of the social structure who is in a position to perceive the sub-structural, or other super-structural, elements of society which *could* be symbolised artistically. His method might be psychologistic—that is, in terms of the individual values and ideas of the artist. It might be crudely structural, without reference to consciousness. The approach proposed here aims to combine the personal and social levels, in a phenomenological but also sociological perspective. The reference, then, will be to ideas, values and meanings, and their expression in art, but the analysis will not remain at the level of biographical explanation. Although any study in the sociology of art, thus conceived, will include reference to the artist himself, this will be within the context of the-artist-in-his-society.

His aesthetically articulated thoughts and feelings are themselves only to be grasped sociologically, and here our earlier comments on the sociology of knowledge and of consciousness demonstrate what is meant by this. But works of art, even within the criteria of investigation which are here being laid down, are often stated to express the societal Zeitgeist—or world-view—a concept which is at once at the level of consciousness, and above the psychological level of the individual artist, and which thus seems to fulfil our requirements. Clearly, too, it seems both a sensible and informative statement to say that a work or a group of works of art reflects the society's collective mind, or the spirit of the age, and yet the concept is open to serious analytical and methodological objections. The next section, therefore, attempts to outline some of these problems.

i The concept of a world-view

The discussion earlier about Schutz's notion of 'multiple realities', in the context of a total Lebenswelt, which existential-phenomenology demonstrates to be an integrated system of meanings,[1] helped us to see how the aesthetic world is related to the world of everyday experience, or common sense, differentiated simply by a mode of attention. This, it should be emphasised, is true in so far as we are considering the Lebenswelt of the individual. Of course, as Schutz and Berger and Luckmann argue, we are already doing sociology in going even so far, by virtue of the *social* origin of many of the definitions and meanings in the individual's existential reality. But the sociology of art which we are considering does not operate on the level of the Lebenswelt of the individual. Rather, it is the meaning-systems of social *groups* which form the background against which the artistic meanings of these groups are to be understood. The phenomenology of a single consciousness is not adequate as an analysis of a collective consciousness.

A critical study of cultural phenomena (art, religion, philosophy) ought to begin by questioning the assumption of cultural unity underlying most work in this field. There is no *a priori* reason why the art forms, myths, political ideologies, etc. of a people at a given period *should* cohere at the level of meaning, or indeed at any level. If it is true to say that in a single individual conflicting meanings cannot co-exist, an extension of this statement to the supra-individual level is not a corollary. The different spheres of meaning might well co-exist, for example, in different sectors of the society, and still be the dominant ideology in that particular sphere. Any conflict might be explained by the fact that one group of society, while not subscribing to what is said to be the religious philosophy of the total group,

[1] Chapter 1, p. 9.

and indeed holding what is seen to be an incompatible artistic ideology, does not entertain an important rival religious philosophy. If
it did, it would be debatable whether the other *is* in fact the religion
of the total group. Perhaps religious meanings are not a part (or
not an important part) of the consciousness of the second group. A
conflict of systems of ideas within a group, then, might be simply a
difference between sections of the group.

Gombrich (1969) questions this assumption of unity generally
made by cultural historians. As he says, 'The assumption is always
that some essential structural similarity must be detected which
permits the interpreter to subsume the various aspects of a culture
under one formula' (p. 32). His critique is of a particular school of
cultural history—the metaphysical history of Hegel and his descen-
dants, in particular Burkhardt, Wölfflin, Lamprecht, Dilthey and
Riegl. The unity of culture in all cases was seen as an expression of
the spirit of the age, manifested in all cultural spheres. Their accounts
were not all as metaphysical as Hegel's, but they were similar in this
basic premiss, for 'all of them felt, consciously or unconsciously, that
if they let go of the magnet that created the pattern, the atoms of past
cultures would again fall back into random dustheaps' (p. 25).

Gombrich does not deny the interconnectedness of the many
different aspects of cultural life. 'Obviously there is something in the
Hegelian intuition that nothing in life is ever isolated, that any
event and any creation of a period is connected by a thousand
threads with the culture in which it is embedded' (p. 30).

But he goes on to say 'It is one thing to see the interconnectedness
of things, another to postulate that all aspects of a culture can be
traced back to one key cause of which they are the manifestations'
(p. 30). 'I see no reason why the study of these connexions should
lead us back to the Hegelian postulates of the Zeitgeist and Volksgeist' (p. 31). His case is that the job of the cultural historian is to
examine in detail the facts in each sphere, and the interconnections,
instead of working with 'the generalizations of Geistesgeschichte', or
attempting to trace the facts back to some postulated common 'spirit
of an age'.

This critique is extremely important, and exposes the fundamental weakness (both epistemological and ontological) of such
cultural history. It deals with the first half of the problem we have
outlined. It stops short of suggesting how one might go about
examining the interconnections across cultural spheres, however;
this, as I see it, is the crucial task of cultural history and the sociology
of culture. It is also the only possible method of returning to the
discredited notion of a cultural unity of some kind, the total ideology
of a social group.

The concept of a 'total ideology' suggests that we turn again to the

57

work of Mannheim for clues as to the unity of cultural systems and the relation between their parts. Besides the essay referred to earlier (p. 46), the relevant work is 'On the interpretation of "Weltanschauung"' (Mannheim 1968). A total ideology, as we have seen, is the Weltanschauung of a group: 'the ideology of an age or of a concrete historico-social group . . . when we are concerned with the characteristics and composition of the total structure of the mind of this epoch or of this group' (Mannheim 1966, pp. 49–50). (The distinction between total and particular ideologies has already been expounded above—chapter 3 (iv).) How is it legitimate to talk about *the* total ideology of a group, for this phrase surely presupposes an unproven unity? Mannheim begins by acknowledging that when we are talking about the total conception of ideology (1966, p. 52),

> we attempt to reconstruct the whole outlook of a social group, and neither the concrete individuals nor the abstract sum of them can legitimately be considered as bearers of this ideological thought-system as a whole. The aim of the analysis on this level is the reconstruction of the systematic theoretical basis underlying the single judgments of the individual. Analyses of ideologies in the particular sense, making the content of individual thought largely dependent on the interests of the subject, can never achieve this basic reconstruction of the whole outlook of a social group. They can at best reveal the collective psychological aspects of ideology, or lead to some development of mass psychology.

So far, Mannheim appears merely to be pointing back to a Hegelian kind of supra-individual entity, and this, as I have argued, is metaphysically unacceptable.

He goes on to discuss the unity of consciousness, and briefly states his acceptance of what is essentially the phenomenology of consciousness (although he does not say this explicitly): 'The philosophy of consciousness has put in place of an infinitely variegated and confused world an organization of experience the unity of which is guaranteed by the unity of the perceiving subject' (p. 58). But how does one step from the guaranteed unity of the total ideology of the individual mind to the unity of the group's ideology? Rejecting both the concepts of 'consciousness as such' and of 'Volksgeist' (the former because it is ahistorical, the latter because it is too inclusive), Mannheim accepts the more specific notion of 'class consciousness' or 'class ideology' (p. 60). He does not go on to prove why an ideology based on class interests is unified throughout its scope and throughout its participants. He makes only the following statement in conclusion (p. 61):

Human affairs cannot be understood by an isolation of their elements. Every fact and event in an historical period is only explicable in terms of meaning, and meaning in its turn always refers to another meaning. Thus the conception of the unity and interdependence of meaning in a period always underlies the interpretation of that period.

But, like Gombrich, he does not demonstrate the nature of this unity and interdependence, neither does he point the way to their exploration.

The earlier essay, 'On the interpretation of "Weltanschauung" ', is more suggestive. The cultural totality of an age, he says, *is* a real entity, for each of the various branches of cultural history (p. 36)

owes its existence to an abstractive operation. None can give a full and valid account of its object within the limits of its own conceptual framework; it will be necessary at some point to refer to the concrete whole itself. . . . Bringing [the] various strata of cultural life in relation to each other, penetrating to the most fundamental totality in terms of which the interconnectedness of the various branches of cultural studies can be understood—this is precisely the essence of the procedure of interpretation which has no counterpart in the natural sciences —the latter only 'explain' things. Thus, even a specialized discipline within the cultural sciences cannot afford to lose sight of the pre-scientific totality of its object, since it cannot comprehend even its narrow topic without recourse to that totality.

He devotes a large section of the essay to an investigation of the nature of that totality and its mode of presentation. First, it is *not* simply an addition of all the separate cultural spheres (p. 42).

Even if we could inventorize all the cultural objectifications of an epoch (we cannot, of course, since the number of items is limitless) a mere addition or inventory would still fall short of that unity we call Weltanschauung. In order to reach the latter, we need a new departure in a different direction, and must perform a mental operation which will be described later, transcending each objectification as something merely itself.

In beginning this operation, he makes the surprising claim that this 'can only be done by phenomenological analysis of the intentional acts directed towards cultural objects' (ibid.), surprising because Mannheim's work and theory on this issue seem to have little to do with the phenomenology of Husserl.

He asks, first, 'whether *Weltanschauung* is a possible object at all, whether, in fact, it is given at all, and in how far the way in which it is given differs from that in which other objects are given to us' (p. 43). To condense his subsequent analysis considerably, his answer is that the Weltanschauung is given *mediately*, through the 'documentary' meaning of particular evidence (as opposed to their 'objective' or 'expressive' meanings) (p. 48).

> The totality we call the 'genius' or 'spirit' (of an epoch) is given to us in this mode of 'documentary' meaning; this is the perspective in which we grasp the elements that go to make up the global outlook of a creative individual or of an epoch.

We grasp the 'classic spirit' or 'Shakespearean spirit' by gathering 'the scattered items of documentary meaning together in over-arching general concepts . . . One may then also define, as a subjective counterpart to these objective cultural generalizations, the corresponding historical subject' (p. 58). He is careful to point out that any such subject is an 'ideal essence', and not an existing empirical group. The collective subjects (unlike those postulated in the case of expressive meaning, which represent the *average* of the group members) are pure constructs (p. 61).

The task Mannheim sets for the sociologist of culture seems to involve a certain methodological circularity, for, to recognise which elements of the factual data are to be taken as documentary evidence, surely we require a prior knowledge of the spirit expressed. Mannheim is explicit about this (pp. 69–70).

> Here there are no parts awaiting integration; on the contrary, something can only be a part by grasped within its appropriate whole. . . . It is the whole which imparts to each fragment its specific function and thereby its meaning and substance.

In the final section of his essay, he discusses how the global outlook can be treated scientifically; it is clear that approaching it via a comprehension of the totality in question is neither a useful nor even a possible method. The crucial question, he says, is 'how the totality we call the spirit, *Weltanschauung*, of an epoch, can be distilled from the various "objectifications" of that epoch' (p. 73), and in answering it can only re-state the circular pattern of understanding (p. 74):

> We understand the whole from the part, and the part from the whole. We derive the 'spirit of the epoch' from its individual documentary manifestations—and we interpret the individual documentary manifestations on the basis of what we know about the spirit of the epoch.

This is essential, and its possibility lies in the fact that 'in the cultural sciences the part and the whole are given simultaneously' (ibid.).

(This is also the basis of the sociology of knowledge of Goldmann and the theory of knowledge of Gadamer, the latter providing a far more thorough analysis and resolution of this paradox. Both of these authors are discussed in later chapters.) But the rest of Mannheim's essay merely proceeds to justify the concept of a Weltanschauung as a scientific entity, and to examine the nature of its expression through its cultural objectifications. Our two central problems remain unsolved, namely: Is it legitimate to talk about such a thing as the world-view of a group, assuming some kind of integration of meanings within it (including the question, what *are* social or societal meanings?)? and How can this world-view be comprehended, given the vicious methodological circle involved? The second question will be dealt with later, in the chapter on Gadamer (chapter 7). The rest of this chapter and the two following chapters will consider various attempts to account for the homogeneity of a Weltanschauung and the nature of social meanings; the chapter on Gadamer will attempt to present a satisfactory method for dealing with the problem, combining the positive features of all these authors, and taking as its starting point Mannheim's hint that only a phenomenological departure will reveal Weltanschauungen.

ii Metalinguistics and the concept of world-view

In chapter 2, I discussed the theories and empirical evidence of metalinguistics, or the theory of linguistic relativity. Returning to language-theory now, we can pursue the question of supra-individual ideologies and meanings through a phenomenon which, because it is clearly *both* an individual and a social entity, suggests itself as the essential mediator between the two levels. The question at issue before was whether and to what extent language structures thought and experience, and thus how much a sociology of knowledge must start with a sociology of language. The general thesis that the construction of reality is at least in some part a linguistic matter was accepted, without going as far as performing a thorough analysis of this process, and it was concluded, somewhat unsatisfactorily, that the sociologist need simply work with a continual awareness of the role of language in the social life of his subjects, and of the potential usefulness of language as a source of methodological hints for his own investigations. In the present context, I am proposing to go back to the fundamental statement of metalinguistic theory and to examine in more detail the place of language in (total) ideology or world-view. Here it is not so much a problem of sociological method, as the epistemological question of what sense we can make of the concept of 'group knowledge'. A thoroughgoing theory of linguistic relativity, if it is acceptable, may provide the necessary bridge from individual to social knowledge; in so far as language is the basis of thought and experience, there ought to be no serious objection to extending our enquiry to social thought and group meanings, for language can be taken for granted as *essentially* a supra-individual phenomenon. Where language is common, therefore, it should follow that thought-patterns and ideologies are common and, furthermore, that there is a guaranteed coherence and unity of the various aspects of ideology even on the group level, since it appears in this light that there is no essential difference between the knowledge of the individual and the knowledge of a social group.

I want to criticise the linguistic-relativity hypothesis here from two points of view. In the first place, it must be admitted that, however formative and pervasive language is in constituting existential reality, pre-linguistic and extra-linguistic ways of experiencing the world must be considered and recognised; on the other hand, so must the possibility of more sophisticated, post-linguistic modes of defining the world. Both of these lie beyond the scope of language itself, and together provide an important reminder that metalinguistics may only be a partial theory of knowledge. Second, the objection can still be made that even here the step from the individual to the group is not as straightforward as it seems; within a phenomenological frame of reference, we still cannot be content with what amounts to a generalisation from the person to the group. These two objections in effect disqualify the theory of language as a contender to serve as the necessary theoretical base of our sociology of knowledge.

I have already discussed the positive contributions of metalinguistic theory, and outlined rather briefly, with reference to complementary work by Berger and Luckmann, Cassirer and others, some of the reasons why its central contentions are correct. In opening our investigations now to other, *non*-linguistic modes of learning and experiencing, I refer back to chapter 2(ii) where, talking about the work of Church, I reported his argument that, with the acquisition of language 'the child undergoes an important change, as a result of which language dominates and transforms his *pre*-verbal experience' (see p. 30). This notion of pre-verbal or 'primitive' (as he also calls it) thought is important, and appears throughout the literature on thought and language, even in the writings of those most committed to the idea of linguistic relativity. A concept of 'pre-linguistic universals', suggesting a certain degree of *non*-relativity of knowledge, can also be found, for example, in Fearing's 'Examination of the conceptions of Benjamin Whorf in the light of theories of perception and cognition' (in Hoijer 1954). Cassirer (1933; 1953) and Dufrenne (1963) both present fascinating theories about the nature of pre-linguistic and non-linguistic experience (both, however, subscribing to the theory that language also structures reality), including explanations of the origin and necessity of language in human life. I do not want to make too much of a diversion here by taking up the question of pre-linguistic experience, but merely to emphasise that language is not the sole precondition and determinant of experience and Weltanschauung. If it is objected that one cannot simply *state* this, without demonstrating the nature and effect of other forms of consciousness and communication which are non-verbal, it can be retorted that neither has it been demonstrated that language is unique or even dominant in the role it has been shown to play in structuring consciousness. This is not just rhetorical quibbling or negative argument. Methodological honesty and the rules of scientific procedure require that we leave open the possibility of non-linguistic factors, as long as neither their existence nor their non-existence has been proved. But it is this very possibility which undermines the importance of metalinguistic theory for anything beyond its own tenets. For it is clear that we cannot be satisfied with a concept of 'knowledge' which is equated simply with language-structured knowledge. The sociology of knowledge and the phenomenology of art and of cultural systems must not restrict itself to such a pre-defined area, as long as other types of 'knowledge' may also exist.

If one *could* somehow reduce the individual's reality to his language system, or to a combination of language and certain other specified factors, would the macro-sociological problem of dealing with social ideologies be any nearer to a solution? In one sense, I think it would be. Language is a perfect mediator between the psychological and sociological levels of analysis; in the study of language, indeed, the two levels can scarcely be kept apart. If a direct and exclusive relationship were demonstrated between language and thought/experience, this would surely be equally valid for the social group. Here the warning must be repeated that there *may* be differences among members of a group which do not occur in one person. Even two people from the same language group can have different ways of using the same language. We might ask how much regional and dialectal discrepancies in speech reflect or reveal mental divergences, or how much Hegelian or Marxist terminology provides a radically new way of looking at the world, even within the same language. I would argue that such differences are potentially enormous when we consider ideologies or world-view. This means then that we must be very aware of what we are taking as a supposedly homogeneous group, as well as deciding what kind and what degree of divergence of language usage, intonation, etc. can safely be ignored in defining such a group. It rather looks as though the theory of language is an unsatisfactory starting-point for a sociology of knowledge. It will only perform this task if one is content with a sociology founded on generalising psychology, and although this is probably both more acceptable and more useful when we are dealing with language than otherwise, it remains a shaky foundation for sociology, both methodologically and epistemologically. Because metalinguistics (like phenomenology, psychology and various other disciplines) starts from the individual, it fails to provide what we are here looking for; namely, a way of grasping the *supra*-individual whole of a cultural system or a societal outlook.

5 Concepts of collective consciousness

Structuralism has the advantage which the discussion so far has found lacking in other schools of thought and theories of society. That is, starting *not* from the individual but from the social structure itself, it is immediately in a position to refer to and consider *social* facts and *group* entities—in this case, of course, total ideologies on the group level. Here I want to consider structuralism and evaluate it as an adequate sociology of culture and, more specifically, of artistic creativity and experience. For if, as it claims, the structural method can reveal the fundamental structure of thought in a given society at a given time, it must certainly be recognised as a serious contender as the essential analytical tool for the apprehension of Weltanschauungen.

Instead of taking structuralism as a single school, I propose to discuss separately two of its chief exponents in social anthropology and sociology, namely Claude Lévi-Strauss and Lucien Goldmann. Structuralism, indeed, is *not* a unified school of thought; different practitioners of the method oppose and debate with one another on its theory and practice. The structural level of analysis also varies enormously, as do the elements of the structure taken as its significant component parts. Lévi-Strauss's structures are kinship systems and myths; Goldmann's are the more Marxist ones of economic (class) structure and superstructure (the 'world vision' of a social group, or the *oeuvre* of a particular writer, etc.). Other structuralists are more interested in psychological, aesthetic and other areas of analysis. (For example, the structural psychoanalysis of Lacan, the semiology of fashion, literature and other intrinsic studies of Barthes, the structural Marxism of Althusser, and the structural philosophy of Foucault.) It is true that many of them are open to the same criticisms, and that from this point of view a general discussion of structuralism as a whole is in order. But if the purpose of this chapter

65

is to evaluate potential contributions to the theory of ideology, this must be undertaken in more specific terms. While all these writers have in common the fact that they start from the postulation of a total coherent structure or of distinct but homologous ones, and while they share, mostly, a vocabulary and method inspired and influenced by the structural linguistics of de Saussure and the Prague school, their interests and practice diverge from this point, making an overall critique of 'structuralism' a necessarily superficial and general exercise. From my limited acquaintance with the writings of structuralists other than Lévi-Strauss and Goldmann, I cannot see that these could be profitably included in this discussion. For the moment, however, I shall waive my earlier (chapter 3(v)) evaluation of the inadequacy of the structural approach to knowledge, in order to examine properly its potential in this respect. I should make it clear in advance that my discussion of these two authors is in no way intended to be exhaustive. I shall only be outlining and examining that part of their work which appears to have a bearing on the problems of this book (without, I hope, distorting their meaning by this selectivity). I do not pretend to evaluate or criticise the respective opus of each in its entirety.

i Lévi-Strauss

The basic premiss of Lévi-Strauss's work, whether on kinship systems, totemism or myths, is that, like language, each of these systems may be taken as a structure, its parts seen in their relationship to each other and to the whole. Thus for example: 'Like phonemes, kinship terms are elements of meaning; like phonemes, they acquire meaning only if they are integrated into systems' ('Structural analysis in linguistics and in anthropology', Lévi-Strauss 1967a, p. 32). In this particular context, Michael Lane's (1970, pp. 13–14) more inclusive discussion of structuralism in general applies equally to the ideas of Lévi-Strauss.

What then are the distinctive properties of structuralism? In the first place it is presented as a method whose scope includes all human social phenomena, no matter what their form, thus embracing not only the social sciences proper (anthropology, sociology, politics, economics and psychology) but also the humanities (literature, history and linguistics) and the fine arts. This is made possible by the belief that all manifestations of social activity, whether it be the clothes that are worn, the books that are written or the systems of kinship and marriage that are practised in any society, constitute languages, in a formal sense. Hence their regularities may be reduced to the same set of abstract rules that define and govern what we normally think of

as language . . . All these social codes are seen to have, like
natural languages, a lexicon, or 'vocabulary'.

Apart from an attempted structural analysis of Baudelaire's poem,
'Les chats', Lévi-Strauss restricts himself to the anthropological
topics referred to above, but he is explicit in insisting that the method
is applicable to modern societies and to other areas of life.

Lane goes on to list the other chief tenets and aspects of the
structural method. These are:

a   The emphasis it gives to wholes, to totalities. 'Its attempt to
study not the elements of a whole, but the complex network of
relationships that link and unite those elements' (p. 14).

b   Its way of seeking structures below or behind empirical reality,
not on the surface, at the level of the observed. By this, Lane appears
to mean that the structuralist investigator goes below the conscious
reality of the subjects themselves, for he quotes Lévi-Strauss here:
'We should not exclude the possibility that the men themselves, who
produce and pass on these myths, *could* be aware of their structure
and mode of operation, though this would not be usual, but rather
partial and intermittent' (Lévi-Strauss 1964).

c   'The essential indivisibility of all the social phenomena
emanating from any given society' (Lane 1970, p. 16). Lane seems
to have condensed his critique of structuralism into a critique of
Lévi-Strauss by now. His point here is that *all* structures in a society
must bear some relation to one another, as they emanate from the
same innate, unconscious structuring capacity. This is the crucial
point I want to take up, for its notion of unconscious mental operations of a society is clearly of interest for our main enquiry.

d   The relations to be observed in any structure are reducible to
binary oppositions (and, Lane could have added, their transformations). Here again it is Lévi-Strauss whom Lane has in mind. This is
obviously an extremely important claim, which can be challenged on
the level of a specific myth dealt with by Lévi-Strauss, on the level of
mythology as an institution, in the context of kinship relations, or
even in the dubious area of the problem of the 'nature of mind', a
pseudo-psychology or metaphysical philosophy which Lévi-Strauss
does not hesitate to enter. However, it is tangential to my central
concern to determine the actual mechanics of the structuring process,
at any level. Furthermore, if our conclusion is that it is both legitimate
and rewarding to look for structures of the kind Lévi-Strauss suggests,
I would be inclined to argue that limiting ourselves to a search for
binary oppositions would both distort the information and narrow
our perception of significant relationships. Lévi-Strauss himself, in
practice, either disregards his own precept (or modifies it, by introducing 'mediating' terms between opposites, for example), or forces

the structure into the pattern in a grotesque manner. (See, for example, the structural analysis of the Oedipus myth, in 'The structural study of myth', Lévi-Strauss 1967a.)

e 'Structuralist analysis is centrally concerned with synchronic as opposed to diachronic structures' (Lane 1970, p. 16). That is, it is ahistorical, or, as Lane prefers to call it, atemporal.

f Related to this point, structuralism is anti-causal (ibid., p. 17). 'The structuralist would argue', says Lane, 'that we can only say that a certain structure is seen to be *transformed* into another structure, and that repeated observations permit us to say that a given structure is always transformed in a particular way, thus giving us not causal laws . . . but laws of transformation' (p. 17).

These and other statements of Lévi-Strauss (and, where relevant, of other structuralists) are each potential points of departure for a general critique of the method. I have mentioned them briefly merely to provide the contextual background to the discussion of a single but fundamental, feature of Lévi-Strauss's theory, and I want to return to this now.

With regard to the injunction to seek structures 'below the surface', Lane proposes the diagram shown in Figure 1 to represent what he interprets (and, I think, quite fairly) as Lévi-Strauss's conception of the nature of social structures.

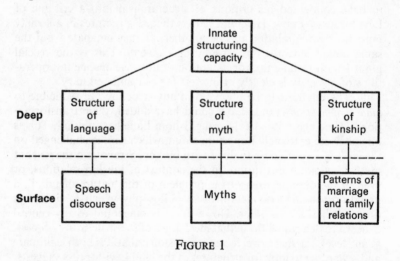

FIGURE 1

Lane then argues (p. 16):

If phenomena are simultaneously created and circumscribed in the way this diagram [Figure 1] suggests, then we would expect to find the homologies, or correspondences in structure, between one aspect of a society, and another, upon which the structuralists have laid such stress.

This is to return to point (c) above. There is no doubt that Lévi-Strauss attributed all empirical structures to the activity of the unconscious mind.

'Kinship systems', like 'phonemic systems', are built by the mind on the level of unconscious thought ('Structural analysis in linguistics and anthropology', Lévi-Strauss 1967a, p. 32).

'Is it language which influences culture? Is it culture which influences language?' But we have not been sufficiently aware of the fact that *both* language and culture are the products of activities which are basically similar. I am now referring to this uninvited guest which has been seated during this Conference beside us and which is the *human mind* ('Linguistics and anthropology', Lévi-Strauss 1967a, p. 70).

Can we conclude that all forms of social life are substantially of the same nature—that is, do they consist of systems of behavior that represent the projection, on the level of conscious and socialized thought, of universal laws which regulate the unconscious activities of the mind? ('Language and the analysis of social laws', Lévi-Strauss 1967a, pp. 57–8).

—a question to which he goes on to suggest an affirmative answer.

If, as we believe to be the case, the unconscious activity of the mind consists in imposing forms upon content, and if these forms are fundamentally the same for all minds—ancient and modern, primitive and civilized (as the study of the symbolic function, expressed in language, so strikingly indicates)—it is necessary and sufficient to grasp the unconscious structure underlying each institution and each custom, in order to obtain a principle of interpretation valid for other institutions and other customs, provided of course, that the analysis is carried far enough (Introduction—'History and anthropology', Lévi-Strauss 1967a, pp. 21–2).

The last two quotations suggest, albeit rather ambiguously, that not only is there a fundamental 'esprit' to be found below the conscious level of a society's manifestations, but that there exists a *universal* unconscious mind, performing similar structuring activities in all societies and through all institutions. Lévi-Strauss's later book, *The savage mind* (1968) is devoted to demonstrating this theory and to exposing the fundamental nature of 'the savage mind', this being 'neither the mind of savages nor that of primitive or archaic humanity, but rather mind in its untamed state, as distinct from mind cultivated or domesticated for the purpose of yielding a return' (Lévi-Strauss 1968a, p. 219). Primarily, its qualities are its aim at analysing and synthesising at the same time; its reciprocity of perspectives in which man and the world mirror each other; its lack of distinction between the moment of observation and that of interpretation; its tendency to totalise. Lévi-Strauss cites art as one zone in which savage thought is still relatively protected, as well as certain (unspecified) sectors of social life. As I have argued above, this step from anthropology or sociology into the speculative domain of the philosophy of mind is quite outside the brief of this study (and, indeed of the work of Lévi-Strauss himself, *qua* anthropologist). At its best, or at least, at its most scientific, such an enquiry can, with some justification, be called psychology; at its most speculative (as is the case with Lévi-Strauss) it is metaphysics. In any case, tentative investigations into the *a priori* nature of mind tell us little or nothing about the more important *a posteriori* contents of a particular mind, or group of minds, in a given society. (It is for similar reasons that my discussion of linguistics and the relation of language and thought did not include Chomsky, who extends linguistic analysis to an analysis of mind itself.) Even the first section of *The savage mind*, comparing modern scientific thought with totemic and primitive thought, and emphasising their similarities rather than their divergences, dilutes the problem by generalising away from the mental facts which concern us. For these, we need to return to Lévi-Strauss's earlier essays, and to remain in the area of particular 'social' or 'group' minds.

In 'Language and the analysis of social laws' (Lévi-Strauss 1967a, pp. 54–65), he draws the following conclusion from the finding that language and kinship are related structures in a society (p. 65).

> The road will then be open for a comparative structural analysis of customs, institutions, and accepted patterns of behavior. We shall be in a position to understand basic similarities between forms of social life, such as language, art, law, and religion, that on the surface seem to differ greatly. At the same time, we shall have the hope of overcoming the opposition between the collective nature of culture and its manifestations in the individual, since the so-called 'collective consciousness' would, in the final analysis, be no more than the expression, on the level of individual thought and behavior of certain time and space modalities of the universal laws which make up the unconscious activity of the mind.

And this, disregarding the arbitrary reference to 'universal laws', is exactly what we have been looking for. Our sociology of culture and of art lacks a method (and even a justification) for comprehending any cultural system as a totality in which to understand its individual elements. Lévi-Strauss's pronouncement promises an even greater possibility, namely a guaranteed manner of grasping the relation of each cultural system to any other, and of all to an underlying 'collective consciousness', or, as we have been calling it, a total ideology. It appears that the possibility of revealing a non-Hegelian group mind has been re-opened. As George Steiner (1970, p. 175) says

> No less than Jung, Lévi-Strauss's studies of magic and myth, of totemism and *logique concrète*, affirm that symbolic representations, legends, image-patterns, are means of storing and conceptualizing knowledge, that mental processes are collective because they reproduce fundamental structural identities.

For Lévi-Strauss, the immense labour of his ethnographic and documentary studies (the *Mythologiques* runs to four volumes) was a necessary undertaking for the main objective of uncovering structures. Only through these structures, arrived at empirically, can the structure of mind be grasped (Schiwy 1969, p. 37).

> Just as the geologist, with his trained eye, can see through the contingencies of a landscape to its basic structures, and just as Marx attempted to discover the ultimately determining base underneath the surface of the social, the young Lévi-Strauss felt called to do the same thing as ethnographer, ethnologist and sociologist. The discovery which determined his life was the existence of an unknown quantity [*unbekannte Grösse*] lending order to the known, an unconscious which confers structure on the conscious, the knowledge that science today must consist precisely in making this unknown known and the unconscious conscious.

Clearly, if there exists something like the collective consciousness which the earlier sections of this book have found problematic, it is more or less this entity, this 'unbekannte Grösse', conceived by Lévi-Strauss. And yet both his conception of this and his limited attempts to grasp it are unsatisfactory. This is partly, it must be admitted, because of the total opposition of point of departure (and, one might say, of ideological tendency) of Lévi-Strauss's structuralism and of the phenomenological sociology of Verstehen. However, I believe our criticism can be more objective than this, and demonstrate at the same time how such a notion of collective consciousness, derived from the type of factual data in question, is necessarily deficient for the purposes of a sociology or philosophy of culture.

In the first place, it is never made clear what kind of mental structure this is, or in what its elements consist. Apart from his very

basic (and therefore not very informative) schema of binary oppositions, Lévi-Strauss nowhere develops a case-study of myth, kinship or
any cultural manifestation into an exposition of the related mental
outlook *apart* from its manifestations. Neither does he indicate how
this might be done. He does present tentative analyses designed to
confirm the homologies across structures (for example, in 'The myth
of Asdiwal', in Leach 1968), or merely to suggest how to look for
such confirmation (e.g. 'Language and the analysis of social laws',
Lévi-Strauss 1967a), but then usually goes on merely to *assert* that
such homologies derive from some underlying mental capacity. As I
have already mentioned, in those cases where he reaches some conclusion about the nature of mind (in *The savage mind*, for example),
or of the particular mind of the society in question, the structure
revealed is so fundamentally simple and bare of content that it really
tells us nothing about what could be called a world-view, but merely
points to one or two formal aspects of its working (if indeed one
accepts even these as convincingly proven). Even the homologies
observed between structures are of the type of simple oppositions, of
spatial relations (high-low, etc.), of simplicity-multiplicity, of number
of elements and complexity of their arrangements.

Second, and this should have become clear in the preceding
paragraphs, Lévi-Strauss's structures are purely *formal*. In describing
any structure, he is not concerned with its content, or the accidental
features through which the structural pattern is observed. This is not
a criticism to be levelled at Lévi-Strauss, since he is perfectly well
aware that this is what his method entails. His insistence on taking
as data the *relations* between terms, and not the terms themselves
('The structural study of myth', Lévi-Strauss 1967a, p. 211), and his
favourite analogy of structures as games, with the structuralist con-
centrating on the *rules* of the game, and not the participants or the
pieces (counters, etc.) in which it is played (see Moore undated)
indicate that his formalism was consciously adopted. (However, mis-
understanding the sense of the accusation of formalism, he is defensive on this question. 'To accuse me of formalism, whereas probably
no other ethnologist has been so attentive to the concrete aspects of
human life!' (quoted by de Gramont 1970, p. 19). This disclaimer is
rather beside the point, as a most rigid formalism can be based on
empirical observations.) It may be that those formal structures of
mind hinted at (but never fully described) by Lévi-Strauss are (a)
possible to discover, (b) interesting, and (c) even informative from
the point of view of some other study. They are not the world-views
sought by cultural analysis.

Finally, I want to take up the issue of Lévi-Strauss's a- or anti-
phenomenological approach. Peter Caws's thesis (1970, pp. 197–214),
is that structuralism, particularly that of Lévi-Strauss, Lacan,

Foucault and Althusser, is an anti-humanism. He refers to the 'absence of the subject' in all these writers (p. 211) (a strange conception indeed in the field of psychoanalysis, but nevertheless a fair description of Lacan's revision of Freud), and argues that 'structuralism is not a humanism, because it refuses to grant man any special status in the world' (p. 204). Caws is not alone in this view of structuralism. Schiwy, for example, says:

> If the essential thing for Sartre is what man makes out of structures, he retains the humanistic position, and does not allow himself to be intimidated by structural a- and anti-humanism. He refuses to reduce man totally to something underlying man, and is convinced 'that man with regard to the structures which condition him is forever "beyond them", for it is something else which allows him to be what he is. Therefore, I do not understand why one should stop at structures: this to me is a logical scandal!'

Caws *is* exceptional in intending his observation as a favourable comment. He sees humanism as 'a detour from which we may be beginning to return to the main track' (p. 209), for humanism is the cause of the central problem of adjustment in modern life, which arises 'out of the invention of the self *as an object of study*' (p. 204). His objection to this, and his faith in the corrective influence of the structural method, are expressed thus (p. 213):

> To restrict the sphere of concern to the human, or even to the living, does not do justice to mind, as its own history has revealed it. The structuring activity that keeps the subject in balance with the world is and must be all-encompassing. To quote Pouillon . . . 'structuralism forbids us to enclose ourselves in any particular reality'.

Its very abdication of an anthropocentric and subjectively-orientated approach is the virtue Caws applauds (p. 210).

> Structuralism, in effect, advocates an engagement with the world, an abandonment of too much self-examination in favor of participation in some significant activity, which in structuring the world will bring the subject into equilibrium with it.

The advantages of structuralism which Caws emphasises are, of course, nothing to do with the methodology of the social sciences, or even the lucrativeness of the method in terms of its results in observed and interpreted data, but consist in the preferability of an attitude, and its consequences for action (political or otherwise) and for living. (It is interesting to note that from a similar critique, Sartre

73

draws a directly opposed conclusion regarding the moral implications for action in structuralism.) Without even meeting Caws's evaluation on its own ground then, I would simply state that I agree entirely with his description of structuralism as anti-humanistic, and go on to lay the blame on this for many of its deficiencies as a theory of society. My argument is that, in abandoning meaning (in the straightforward sense of subjective meaning to a person or persons, and not any derivative concept such as the non-personal 'meaning', that is, 'significance' or 'relationship', of a fact in its social structure), structural analysis, and any social science, relinquishes its opportunity to perceive the relations between the various spheres of social life, and between each of these and the *totality* of social experience. I hesitate to pursue this argument to its extreme, however. Just as it can hardly be denied that a non-semantic linguistics is both possible and productive, however one evaluates the nature of its results, so, analogously, can there be no *a priori* objection to a structural anthropology or any other discipline, which defines its units and its structures without any reference to meaning. In a sense then, both Lévi-Strauss and his critics are right in their dialogue, given their disparate interests in the subject-matter. Nevertheless, in examining one particular critic's attack on this subject, I conclude by recommending once again the maintenance of the discussion on the level of meaning.

Paul Ricoeur has challenged structuralism on several occasions. Here I am concerned with his arguments in the article 'Structure et herméneutique' (1963a) and in his dialogue with Lévi-Strauss ('Réponses à quelques questions' 1963b). It is here that he raises the question of meaning, and confronts Lévi-Strauss with the problems inherent in his method, arising from its operation independently of Verstehen. He begins his article with the direct accusation that structuralism is non-hermeneutic and anti-phenomenological. The hermeneutic method consists in understanding the other and his signs and symbols by a simultaneous understanding of oneself and of being. 'It is the function of hermeneutics to make the comprehension of the other—and of his signs in multiple cultures—coincide with the comprehension of oneself and of being' (p. 617). Structuralism, on the other hand, operates with a clear distinction of structure from researcher (pp. 596-7).

> Just as structuralism aims to place at a distance, to objectivate, to separate from the personal equation of the researcher, the structure of an institution, a myth, a rite, so hermeneutic thought immerses itself in what has been called 'the hermeneutic circle' of understanding and belief, which disqualifies it as science and qualifies it as meditative thought.

And (p. 600)

> It is a question . . . of a system of categories without reference
> to a thinking subject; this is why structuralism, as a philosophy,
> will develop a type of intellectualism which is thoroughly
> anti-reflexive, anti-idealist, anti-phenomenological.

Furthermore, structuralism, with its emphasis on *relations* between
parts rather than on the content of a structure itself, opts for syntax
against semantics ('je caractérisai d'un mot la méthode: c'est un
choix pour la syntaxe contre la sémantique', p. 607), a mistaken
restriction of investigation even in the case of totemism and primitive
societies, and one which is many times compounded, according to
Ricoeur, when one turns to complex and modern societies. In these,
content is crucially significant, and hermeneutic knowledge is necessary, interpreting the content itself (p. 608).

> At the other pole of mythical thought, of which I shall give a
> few examples in a moment, taken from the hebrew world,
> structural understanding is perhaps less important, and certainly
> less exclusive, and more manifestly needs to be articulated on a
> hermeneutic understanding which attempts to interpret the
> contents themselves, in order to prolong their life and
> incorporate their efficacy in philosophical reflection.

Considering the Hebraic biblical tradition, instead of primitive
mythology, Ricoeur argues that the structural method does not
exhaust the sense of symbols, but leaves a *surplus of meaning* ('un
surplus de sens', p. 614). And since in this case meaning is meaning
in a historical tradition, only a hermeneutic, not a structural,
comprehension can take into account the diachronic element. The
very lack of subject-centredness which Caws had applauded is
criticised by Ricoeur in his famous labelling of structuralism as a
Kantianism without a transcendental subject (p. 618).

> Lacking that structure of reception, which I myself conceive as
> a mutual articulation of reflection and hermeneutics, structuralist
> philosophy seems to me to be condemned to oscillate between
> several approximations to philosophy. One could call it a
> Kantianism without a transcendental subject, or an absolute
> formalism, which would establish even the correlation of nature
> and culture.

This comment is made, I think, with particular reference to *The
savage mind*, where Lévi-Strauss turns to the fundamental categories
of mind, but is applicable, certainly in its charge of formalism, to the
rest of Lévi-Strauss's work. Lévi-Strauss himself accepts this definition with no particular objections (1963, p. 633):

75

I am completely in agreement with M. Ricoeur when he defines my position—no doubt to criticise it—as 'a Kantianism without a transcendental subject.' This deficiency causes him certain reservations, whereas nothing prevents me from accepting his formulation.

Ricoeur concludes with something of a compromise, for just as the apprehension of structural homologies presupposes a hermeneutic grasp of meaning, so, he finds, there can be no grasp of meaning without a minimum comprehension of structures, for a symbol alone *has* no meaning. In short then, 'The primary thing is the semantic constitution in the form of "similar-dissimilar", at the root of symbols or figuratives. From this a syntax of arrangements of signs at many levels can be elaborated in abstract form' (p. 626). Considering Lévi-Strauss, indeed, Ricoeur reminds us that his formalism is not as absolute as the theory has it (apparently contradicting his own earlier statement) (pp. 622–3).

A careful examination of *The savage mind* suggests that one can always find, behind the homologies of structure, semantic analogies which make the various levels of reality comparable, whose 'code' assures their convertibility . . . Structural understanding never proceeds without a degree of hermeneutic intelligence, even if the latter is not thematized.

In perceiving the structural homology of systems he asks 'Isn't the objective science of exchanges an abstract segment in the total comprehension of symbolic function, which is basically semantic comprehension?' (p. 604). Hermeneutics, of course, is not the same thing as phenomenology. In a later chapter, I shall discuss in some detail the relationship of the two, and the nature and value of the step from phenomenology to hermeneutics. Ricoeur uses both words without actually defining them, except to say of hermeneutics (p. 621)

the interpretation of a transmitted meaning consists in the conscious recovery of a symbolic depth, overdetermined by an interpretation which places itself in the same semantic field as that which it understands, and thus enters into the 'hermeneutic circle'.

To simplify the philosophical intricacies for the present purpose, we can say that his conception of a method supported in opposition to Lévi-Strauss's structuralism, is a variant of the method of Verstehen, by which the social scientist has access to the *semantics* of observed behaviour patterns and institutions, myths and literary traditions. (The additional philosophical notion of self-understanding through the hermeneutic process need not be considered here.) Before judging the validity and relevance of Ricoeur's comments, in the light of our own objective, I shall look briefly at Lévi-Strauss's own reply to his critics ('Réponses à quelques questions', 1963), including Ricoeur, who here repeats some of the arguments contained in his essay. To the suggestion that only a semantic understanding of meaning is adequate in many cases, Lévi-Strauss replies that we cannot understand things both from the outside and from the inside, and, indeed, that we cannot understand from the inside at all unless we were *born* inside (p. 637). The transporting of consciousness, in the way hermeneutics, verstehende sociology and phenomenology advocate, is for Lévi-Strauss 'compromised from the start' ('d'avance compromise', p. 637). And not only is this not possible; fortunately it is not even necessary, for in his view meaning is reducible, and thus is never the primary phenomenon. 'From my point of view, meaning is never a primary phenomenon: meaning is always reducible. In other words, behind all meaning there is non-meaning, and the opposite is not the case. For me signification is always phenomenal' (p. 637). This is an extremely provocative assertion, and in fact Lévi-Strauss retreats somewhat under pressure from Mikel Dufrenne (pp. 639–40).

I am in no way excluding—it would indeed be impossible—that recovery of meaning which M. Ricoeur refers to; perhaps the difference lies in the fact that, for me, it appears as a supplementary means which can be dispensed with when we are trying to control the validity of our syntactic operations after the event . . . The recovery of meaning seems to me secondary and derivative, from the point of view of method, in relation to the essential task which consists in taking apart the mechanism of objective thought.

Meaning is recognised as an autonomous sphere of social life, and its limited relevance to sociological and anthropological enquiry is reluctantly conceded; Ricoeur and Dufrenne will not be satisfied, however, until they have converted Lévi-Strauss to the revolutionary (in terms of change of standpoint) view that meaning is central to social life, and primary in its analysis and exploration. Ricoeur proposes with confidence the possibility of a collaboration, an 'articulation', of hermeneutics with structuralism, for, unlike other critics, he does not condemn the structural method as intrinsically inimical to the inclusion of meaning (Ricoeur 1963a, pp. 620–7).

Turning the objections of Ricoeur and Dufrenne to account in the resumption of our own line of enquiry, my contention here is that the phenomenological bias and hermeneutic approach found lacking in the structuralism of Lévi-Strauss can be the key to the solution of the problem both of the nature of a total world-view, a collective consciousness, and of the relation of systems of art to this world-view.

I re-emphasise a certain neutrality in the debate at this point: lack of attention to meaning does *not* seem to me to invalidate the structural method and the copious works of structuralist writers. As in linguistics, purely syntactical analysis can be a legitimate science. (Cf. here my analogous comments on the anti-subjectivism and disregard of meaning of behaviouralism and positivism in the social sciences, in chapter 1.) What I am arguing, rather, is that only by opting for semantics over and above syntactics can the particular weaknesses of the method, referred to above, be surmounted, and the positive contributions of Lévi-Strauss adopted for a wider sociology of culture. In putting meaning before other structural facts, I am by no means excluding Lévi-Strauss's 'unconscious structures' of the mind to restrict the dialogue to conscious meanings and overt attitudes alone, for this would certainly be to impoverish the available phenomena and lessen our chances of grasping significant meaning structures. As Mannheim has pointed out, total ideologies are for the most part unconscious themselves. In any case, we ought not to prejudice the possibility of discovering systems of meaning, whether the Lebenswelt of the individual or the Weltanschauung of a group, by defining in advance their supposed level of consciousness.

From our reading of Lévi-Strauss, we have drawn the important recognition of the homology of diverse structures in a given society, and the tentative hypothesis that these find their common ground, and perhaps their origin, in the more basic mental structure of the social group. Unlike the theory of metalinguistics (chapter 4(ii)), Lévi-Strauss's theory does not limit his concept of a collective consciousness to a purely linguistic creation, but leaves open the question of its origin and its constituting features. The next step is to go further in the direction of describing this collective consciousness, and its manifestations in the different spheres of life, rejecting both the formalism of Lévi-Strauss and his reduction of the whole question to a simple, fundamental principle of binary oppositions and their transformations. We need to be able to discover something more concrete in each particular case, a richer and more suggestive concept of a world-view. Moreover, whether we grasp art, myths, kinship systems, etc., as structures or not, we require some method of determining what to take as the units of analysis, which may in turn be related to elements (or, of course, relations) of the underlying structure. I hope that the following pages of this book will continue to work towards an adequate theory, pointing out what is absent in the writings of the authors considered, and pursuing the enquiry where they have stopped short. Lévi-Strauss has presented us with the possibility of an entity which could be called a collective consciousness, and which does not rely on metaphysics or dubious ontology, as for example Hegel's Geist or Spirit does. His analysis of this mental existent is far from satisfactory, however, as is his evidence that it is in some way related to what Lane calls the 'surface structures' of society. Taking our direction from Ricoeur's criticisms, our attempt at a solution to the dilemma will be based on the connection *through meaning* of all the diverse spheres of social life.

ii Goldmann

'Lévi-Strauss . . . is the exponent of a formalistic system that tends to eliminate in a radical way all interest in history and the problem of meaning.' This is Goldmann's criticism of Lévi-Strauss's structuralism (Goldmann 1969a, p. 12), and his own version of structuralist sociology claims to take account of both these crucial factors. As I have argued, it is particularly his disregard of the problem of meaning which prevents Lévi-Strauss from developing an adequate model for the study and comprehension of the various structures of social life and the fundamental structure of the collective consciousness. Goldmann succeeds in demonstrating both how structuralism may become a more sophisticated, phenomenological method, and also how a concept of world-views or world visions forms part of the theory.

He makes clear his allegiance to Verstehen-sociology in the same essay (1969a, p. 32).

One of the principal merits of phenomenology and of the Gestalt school of psychology has been to remind us of the importance of this distinctively human awareness and of the meanings which acts and events have for it. In this sense, to study history is first of all to try to *understand* men's actions, the impulses which have moved them, the ends which they have pursued, and the meaning which their behaviour and their actions had *for them*.

(He goes on, however, to postulate another level of meaning which must be recognised, and which phenomenology ignores (ibid., pp. 32–3).

The weakness of phenomenology seems to us to lie precisely in the fact that it limits itself to a comprehensive description of the facts of consciousness (or, to be more exact, of their 'essence'). The real structure of historical facts permits, however, beyond the *conscious* meaning of those facts in the thought and intentions of the actors, the postulation of an objective meaning which often differs from the conscious meaning in an important way.

Whether this *is* in fact something of an entirely different nature from the meanings uncovered by phenomenology is something worth discussing, although it hardly affects the present discussion of Gold-mann's work.)

I am taking my summary of Goldmann's theory from the following of his writings: *The hidden god*; *Pour une sociologie du roman*; *The human sciences and philosophy*; 'Sociology of literature—status and problems of method' (*ISSJ* 1967a); and 'Ideology and writing' (*TLS* 1967b). His main interest, of course, is in the sociology of literature, but his structuralism is just as much a general theory of society as that of Lévi-Strauss, for his thesis is that the relevant structures in literature originate in the *mental* structures, or world visions, of a group in society, structures which one might also expect to find expressed in other forms of life in that society. In effect, his genetic structuralism is a synthesis of structuralist theory with a traditional sociology of knowledge. Both he and Lévi-Strauss purport to be Marxists. In the case of Lévi-Strauss, the claim is rather hard to defend against more or less orthodox Marxist critics. The structures of myth, kinship and totemic systems, all belonging to the ideational sphere of the superstructure, are barely traced to their material sub-struc-ture; where this is attempted, it is done in a very vague and per-functory way, almost *en passant*. The accent is on the non-material factors. As Lévi-Strauss never pretends that his structuralism is genetic, perhaps he cannot be accused of anti-Marxism or idealism, for analysis of the superstructure alone neither asserts nor denies any relationship to the sub-structure, whereas a theory purporting at the same time to explain the *origin* and *genesis* of these structures must make explicit its commitment or non-commitment to Marxism. Nevertheless, there is not much evidence in Lévi-Strauss's anthro-pological work to suggest that he *is* a Marxist; if he is, the commit-ment is not apparent in, and thus, not relevant to, his academic work. And, one might add, his writings are not grounded in *any* sociology of knowledge, Marxist or otherwise. Where he does relate the struc-ture of a myth to something which could be considered a more fundamental or determining structure, he usually expresses the relationship as nothing stronger than one of homology. (Here I am ignoring his later ideas about the fundamental nature of mind, and the manifestation of its operations on the level of, for example, totemic classification. As I argued earlier, this part of Lévi-Strauss's work is neither sociology nor anthropology, but pseudo-psychology and rather dubious philosophy.)

Goldmann, on the other hand, is primarily a sociologist of know-ledge, and indisputably a Marxist one; only secondarily is he also a structuralist. His objective is to demonstrate the genesis of literary and philosophical ideas in material, particularly class, factors, and his method is to comprehend these various factors in their relevant structural contexts. The mediating concept between social base and ideational (literary, philosophical) systems is the world-view or world vision. This is seen as a coherent totality, common to the members of a social group. It is not *all* social groups whose mental structures constitute world-views, however, but only privileged groups, whose social needs produce a total view of human life. 'This structuration can only be attached to groups *whose consciousness tends towards a global vision of man*' (Goldmann 1969b, p. 348). In Goldmann's view these groups, historically, have always been social classes. 'From the point of view of empirical research, it is certain that, for a very long period, social classes have been the only groups of this type' (ibid., see also Goldmann 1969a, pp. 127–8).

Other groupings, he argues, cannot explain the *essential* structure of a work of art, for example, but only its peripheral elements. (However, in his later writings, he seemed to be beginning to concede the possibility of the equal importance of other groupings, such as the French radical left. See Mackie 1970.) Elsewhere, he makes it clear that the 'privileged' position of social classes is an empirical fact, and neither a logical one nor a mere prejudice (1969a, pp. 101–2).

As partisans of historical materialism, we see the existence of social classes and the structure of their relations (struggle, equilibrium, collaboration according to country and historical period) as the key phenomena for the understanding of social reality past and present. And we see them in this way, not for dogmatic reasons of faith or because of preconceived ideas but, quite simply, because our own research, as well as the studies with which we have been able to acquaint ourselves, have almost always shown us the outstanding importance of this social group in comparison with all others.

Thus, in his own study of the tragic vision, expressed in the *Pensées* of Pascal and the tragedies of Racine (Goldmann 1964), he finds the social co-ordinates of that world vision in the class structure of the period, re-affirming at the outset that this is the most important group to which an individual may belong, 'from the point of view of intellectual and artistic activity and creation' (p. 16). Here, we are given a very brief explanation of why this should be the case (pp. 16–17).

Up to the present day, it is class, linked together by basic economic needs, which has been of prime importance in influencing the ideological life of man, since he has been compelled to devote most of his thought and energy either to finding enough to live on or, if he belonged to a ruling class, to keeping his privileges and administering and increasing his wealth.

(Clearly such a simplistic notion of class structure is questionable, particularly if it is intended to apply to the contemporary situation, and I shall suggest later that class itself is too narrow a concept of important social groupings.)

World visions, then, originate in certain social groups, and are in some way related to their needs and aspirations. Goldmann also refers to them as collective consciousnesses (1969a, p. 128; 1969b, p. 366; 1964, p. 18). Both these notions, as we have seen, are subject to ontological and epistemological debate. Goldmann pre-empts attack by avoiding the two major pitfalls. That is, he perceives that any so-called 'consciousness' must have a subject, and a non-metaphysical subject at that, and supplies this under the name of the 'trans-individual subject' (1967b). At the same time, he denies the charge of psychologism, arguing that the transindividual subject is not a generalisation, or even an ideal type, based on an *actual* individual, but has an identity of its own (1969b, p. 339).

> One can, then, and this is the case with dialectical, Hegelian and especially Marxist thought, admit with romanticism the collectivity as a real subject, without, however, forgetting that this collectivity is nothing other than a complex network of inter-individual relations.

The transindividual subject comes into existence with any social, that is, inter-individual, action, and is in fact the sum of the actors involved (1967b). Goldmann is careful to point out here that the consciousness of the transindividual subject has no reality of its own, but exists only in the individual consciousnesses involved. If this is so (and it surely cannot be otherwise), the firm insistence on the distinction between individual and transindividual consciousness seems exaggerated, for we could say that the collective or transindividual consciousness exists in the minds of individuals by virtue of their social situation. The point appears to be, however, that the collective consciousness, although it can be discovered as a total, coherent view, does not necessarily exist in this form in any one of the actual individuals of the group. It is for this reason that its 'subject' (which is in fact a nominal or logical subject only) is given a defining name, implying its non-identity with the individual subject. But this means that once again one is faced with the problem of explaining the cohesion of a world-view, and justifying the assumption that such a total structure exists, without an existent subject to guarantee unity. This is where Goldmann's reliance on what we might call philosophical structuralism provides the missing link in the argument. All human activity is structured, says Goldmann, and is 'significative', in that it is an attempt to resolve a practical problem (1967b; 1969b, p. 338). Indeed, he seems at times to equate 'structure' with 'significance'; the structuration of an action or of anything experienced lies essentially in its signification. I cannot find a place where Goldmann actually defines 'structure', although on the whole it looks like the concept we are familiar with from reading Lévi-Strauss and other writers: namely, a total, self-contained entity, whose parts are interrelated and which forms some sort of a coherent whole. On the other hand, it is clear that when Goldmann talks about the 'structured character of activity' he means the *significance* of that activity. Is this a real ambiguity, or even a loose, imprecise use of terms, with critical consequences for the theory itself? I think the connections can be supplied for Goldmann in this case, even though he himself does not make them explicitly. When we accept that significance is necessarily significance *within* a structure, it is clear that to say that human activity is significant is also to say that it is a part of a structure. In my discussion of phenomenological philosophy above this was exactly what I was arguing, when I said that meaning only exists in a context. If an activity, or anything else, is significant for the individual, then that is to say that it is or becomes part of his mental structure (Gestalt). If I am right in attributing to Goldmann this belief in necessary structuration (and he gives no other reason for stating that all activity is structured), then the relation between meaning and structure is exactly that perceived by Gestalt psychology and existential phenomenology. (As a possible confirmation of this interpretation, we may note the following short extract from 'Ideology and writing' (1967b), which still does not go much further either in defining the terms or in making explicit the relationship:

> Every human fact is significative; . . . this significance derives from its character of relative totality (or, what comes to the same thing, of 'structure'), and can only be brought out clearly by being introduced into a structure of which it forms part or with which it is identified . . . Significative structures are the result of a *genesis* and cannot be understood or explained independently of this genesis.

This much we had already established by a simpler phenomenological sociology. It is the move from individual to transindividual subject which is interesting, for Goldmann affirms equal structuredness in the consciousness of the latter. Given that the world-view of the individual, and therefore anything within his experience, is structured at the level of meaning (i.e. in that it is necessarily significative), we want to know whether we should expect a similar structural unity in the collective consciousness, and if so, as Goldmann states, *why* this should be the case. The answer cannot be that the transindividual consciousness, which Goldmann has admitted can only exist in individual consciousnesses, is thus equivalent to an individual consciousness, because we have also noted that it may not exist in its totality in *any one* individual subject. Here again, we can only suggest an answer which Goldmann himself never made explicit. The clue lies in his non-reified understanding of structures. Unlike the structuralism of Lévi-Strauss and other writers, he says (1967b),

> genetic structuralism, which has long been stressing the essential importance of structures in understanding history must now defend the existence of the transindividual subject, the fact that the structure is not an autonomous and active entity which holds man prisoner, but an *essential characteristic* of the activity of a subject (individual-libido or transindividual) who alone is active and creative, and to a lesser extent, the fact that, although no human activity can be understood outside the structures that govern it (language, relations of production, social groups, world-view, etc.), these structures are themselves the result of man's earlier praxis, that is, the praxis of the subject, and will be in turn modified by the present praxis, of which they constitute an *essential characteristic* and not an external datum.

Genetic structuralism never abandons (1967b)

> either the existence of the subject or the structured character of all its activities, or the existence of activities with an individual subject (libido), or of activities with transindividual subjects (history, economics, social life, culture), or their permanent interaction.

In other words, structures are simply products of historical subjects; furthermore, history is a continual process of structuration and destructuration. (This dialectical view of structure and the individual can be compared with Berger and Luckmann's analysis of the processes of creation, objectification and reification, Berger and Luckmann 1967.)

Since all structures originate in the praxis of a subject, and since all praxis is significative, the same significations must be visible in those structures, even where they are far removed (historically) from their constituting praxis. (This is not, it should be emphasised, to pre-judge the important issue as to whether such significance was or is conscious or unconscious, manifest or latent.) But on the problem of coherence of a structure, all one can say is that inasmuch as a social group is cohesive and unified, its mental structures will be similarly so. The more complex its composition, and the greater the number of diverse elements making it up, the smaller the chance that the structures originating in its past activity will approximate to a single totality, a Gestalt, which would be a structure, rather than a conglomeration of structured elements. Goldmann recognises this divergence of most world-views from the ideal of a structured whole (1969b, p. 346):

> Without exception, however, these tendencies remain far from effective coherence to the extent that they are, as we have already argued, opposed in the consciousness of individuals by the membership of each of them in numerous other social groups.

In fact, this is sufficient for Goldmann's sociology of knowledge. He allows for 'structures' which are not unified and total systems; as we have seen, he maintains that only certain groups, whose identity is most strictly determined, such as classes, have the global mental structure which he calls a world vision. Where group interests are strongest, and most influential in directing activity and structuring meaning, and where, *a fortiori*, all members of the group are alike in structuration of consciousness the transindividual subject will not vary much from activity to activity, or in its actual constitution in members of the group from time to time, for the active consciousness will remain more or less constant in its essential features.

This collective consciousness reaches its height in the 'exceptional individual' (Goldmann 1964, p. 18; 1969b, p. 346), as well as in situations where pressures to group identification are strongest (e.g. class conflict). When the exceptional individual happens to be a writer, his work is the direct expression of the world vision of his class, or other social group. When Goldmann says that a cultural work always has a *collective* subject (1967a), he means that the writer's consciousness coincides with the world vision of his group, and that more or less identical structures will be found in his work, in the world vision itself, and in the social situation which gave rise to both of these. Elsewhere he says (1969a, p. 129)

> A mode of behaviour or a text becomes an expression of collective consciousness only to the extent that the structure which it expresses is not peculiar to its author but is shared by the various members who form the social group.

The relation of literary structure to world vision, and to social base, is one of homology (1969b, p. 41).

> The relationship between collective thought and great individual literary, philosophical, theological, etc. creations does not reside in any identity of content, but in a more extended coherence and in a homology of structures, which can be expressed in imaginary content quite different from the real content of the collective consciousness.

This is the essence of Goldmann's sociology of literature, then; a

85

homology of social structure and literary creation, mediated by the world vision. The problem of Gestalt on all these levels is solved not by theory or empirical observation, but by definition, for only unified and homogeneous groups have coherent and unified world-views, and only such world-views, through the agency of the exceptional individual (the incarnation of the transindividual subject?), find their expression in a body of artistic work. There is no question of proving that all social groupings are cohesive, or that all world-views or literary works are necessarily significant structures. There is no need to demonstrate a 'psychic structure which is common to a very great extent' to individuals of a group (1969a, p. 127), when we choose as relevant groups for examination *only* those groups where the psychic structure *is* common to a very great extent.

The relevance of Goldmann for our work is twofold. In the first place, his is a serious and considerable attempt to confront the problem of the supra-individual subject, with its related concepts of group mind, world vision, and social meanings. These are all notions which we have found central in a sociology of knowledge, and which have always presented themselves as problematic, and have been unsatisfactorily resolved by most sociologists. In the second place, our ultimate purpose in this enterprise is to develop, from a wider sociology of knowledge, a sociology of art and literature, and Goldmann demonstrates, in theory and in his own research, how this can be achieved. Clearly many of the deficiencies of Lévi-Strauss's structuralism are removed in the process, and I think it must be acknowledged that both as a sociology of knowledge and as a structuralist theory, Goldmann's work has many merits. It is, indeed, the closest we have come to an adequate sociology of knowledge. Here I shall not discuss or criticise it from the narrower point of view of a sociology of literature (questioning his conception of literature, for example, the kind of works he regards as significant, or the level of analysis at which he considers these works of literature). Following the general line of argument of this book, Goldmann is here under evaluation in the related but wider and preliminary debate over the validity of assuming a unified Weltanschauung of a group, and the sense (or non-sense) of talking about social or societal phenomena in the language of psychology and the philosophy of mind.

It will help us to assess Goldmann's contribution to the kind of theory we are trying to develop if we briefly redefine the latter at this point. A verstehende sociology of art, we have argued, has the dual advantage of comprehending works of art in their own (artistic or aesthetic) terms, and of comprehending them in their relationship to social life in general. It faces the problem, as soon as it moves, as sociology, from the particular artist and his social context to talking more generally about the productions of a society, or defining both the relevant social group and the relevant set of works of art, and of explaining (within a theory at the level of meaning) in what sense art can be said to be the expression of such a group. The introduction of the concept of structure gives us a potentially important tool for this analysis, and in the hands of Goldmann, the tool is employed without sacrificing the fundamental perspective of meaning. Social groups are defined, in accordance with Marxian tradition, by their self-consciousness and their needs and purposes. The world vision of a group with its logical 'transindividual' subject and its concretion in the exceptional individual, is identified and given a non-metaphysical sense. And the sociology of knowledge is extended to a sociology of literature by virtue of philosophical structuralism; that is, the theory that all human behaviour is structured, and that the structures of the various spheres of social life and expression of a group are related in a homology of form.

I have already suggested that the limitation imposed on the theory by insisting on the uniqueness of economic class as the origin of a world vision is one of the main defects in Goldmann's theory. In those later essays where he relaxes this formulation, allowing the possible importance of non-economic groups, such as those united by ideological interests, the problem then becomes one of knowing *which* groups to take as creators of world visions. This is something Goldmann never manages to explain. Therefore, once we admit that class is not necessarily a group, or the only group, with the unity of purpose and identification which gives rise to a world vision, we need some way of identifying such groups. Second, this type of sociology of literature is also unnecessarily restricted in that it is *only* those single-purpose, unified groups which Goldmann argues alone create a total world vision, which are to be taken as structural units in practice. Each individual is a member of many different groups—economic, social, professional, ideological, racial, religious—and it is equally valid to trace his philosophical views and his artistic creations to any one of these, or to their combination. It may be true, as Goldmann argues, that these rarely form a global vision of man (although they *may* do so, and although class, on the other hand does not necessarily do so). But Goldmann goes on to rule such groups out of a sociology of knowledge and of literature, maintaining that *only* those groups whose consciousness tends towards a global vision of man are structured and create structures (1969b, p. 348). I should like to argue that a more sophisticated structural sociology should be able to take account of a variety of social groupings, and their expression in ideology and art, and it should also be able to refer to the total society, with its complex of overlapping and opposing groups. Literature may be the expression of group conflict, resulting from membership in more than one group, with divergent interests. The exceptional individual must not be seen as merely the purest exponent of the philosophy of a single, simple group. This means we are faced with the choice of either starting from the work of the individual writer/artist, and relating it, in structure and/or content, to his complex social situation, his position in numerous groups, or elaborating a macro-theory of society and literature, sophisticated enough to incorporate the diversity of a modern society. Goldmann rightly sees the problems a structural sociology faces, once it abandons the simpler view of a single group, single structure, single world vision, for the prerequisite for structural analysis is a structural whole, definable and self-contained. Recognising the originality and importance of Goldmann's structural sociology of literature, we see as our task an extension of his theory into a more inclusive sociology, which, without relinquishing either the structural or the verstehende perspective, does not necessarily limit itself to class or other single-group analysis. In a later chapter, I shall consider the possibility of such a total sociological theory, in the context of Gadamer's hermeneutics, and the limitations we have pointed out in Goldmann's work will, as far as is possible, be removed.

6 Concepts of collective consciousness (continued)

In this chapter, I want to consider the sociological theory of Durkheim and its critique and revision in the structural-functionalism of Talcott Parsons. Like structuralism, these theories have the advantage which comes from working with a sociological perspective; that is, they are not required to create social facts out of psychological or individual facts, by addition, extension, generalisation or less legitimate means. Perhaps the most famous of Durkheim's precepts to the sociologist was to 'consider social facts as things' (Durkheim 1938, p. 14). Parsons, for his part, insists on the autonomy of society, personality and culture, despite their complex interrelationship. Further, we find in both authors a concept more or less equivalent to the 'world-view' or 'total ideology' which has been under discussion here: in the case of Durkheim, this, of course, is the *conscience collective*, and in the case of Parsons, it is the cultural system itself, and more specifically that part of it comprising patterns of value-orientation. Looking at each of these authors in turn, I shall examine these concepts, and consider their relevance for this essay.

iii Durkheim

In *The division of labour in society* (1947), Durkheim defines the *conscience collective* thus (pp. 79–80):

> The totality of beliefs and sentiments common to average citizens of the same society forms a determinate system which has its own life; one may call it the *collective* or *common conscience*. No doubt, it has not a specific organ as a sub-stratum, it is, by definition, diffuse in every reach of society. Nevertheless, it has specific characteristics which make it a distinct reality. It is, in effect, independent of the particular conditions, in which individuals are placed; they pass on and it remains. . . . It is the psychical type of society, a type which has

its properties, its conditions of existence, its mode of development, just as individual types, although in a different way.

In this early work, Durkheim argues that, with the increasing division of labour, the collective conscience grows weaker (p. 283), and the nature of society is transformed from one based on mechanical solidarity to one based on organic solidarity, with parallel changes in the nature of law and punishment, from repressive to co-operative, or restitutive. Thus, where labour is not yet divided (p. 109),

> there exists a social solidarity which comes from a certain number of states of conscience which are common to all the members of the same society. This is what repressive law materially represents, at least in so far as it is essential.

But in societies characterised by organic solidarity, the collective conscience decreases in extent and in strength, and becomes more general and vague in content, allowing the place of the individual in society to grow in importance. For where the collective conscience is at its strongest, where it 'completely envelops our whole conscience and coincides in all points with it . . . at that moment, our individuality is nil' (p. 130). Durkheim's first description of the *conscience collective*, then, shows it as those beliefs and feelings held in common by the members of a society. Moreover, as Parsons points out, the emphasis is on the ethical or value character of the *conscience collective* (Parsons 1949, p. 318). Durkheim does not make this explicit, but when he says that punishment is the 'avenge of outrage to morality', and elsewhere calls it the resistance of the common conscience (p. 103), it is clear that he either equates morality with the common conscience or sees the former as the most important part of the latter.

In *Suicide* and *Rules of sociological method*, the emphasis is still on the moral or normative nature of the collective conscience. Anomie can thus be seen as freedom from the collective conscience (see Parsons 1949, p. 336). Here Durkheim pursues the question of the nature of social facts, and, particularly in the *Rules*, insists on their autonomous existence, independent of the individual. 'Society is not a mere sum of individuals. Rather, the system formed by their association represents a specific reality which has its own characteristics' (Durkheim 1938, p. 103). 'The social fact is a thing distinct from its individual manifestations' (ibid., p. 7). The important rule which follows from this, therefore, is that the sociologist must abandon psychology, and take the social facts themselves as his data (ibid., p. 111). 'If . . . we begin with the individual, we shall be able to understand nothing of what takes place in the group. In a word, there is between psychology and sociology the same break in continuity as between biology and the physicochemical sciences' (ibid., p. 104).

This means, with regard to the *conscience collective*, that it too is something to be approached directly, and not discovered in the individual consciousnesses of the members of a group. 'A social fact', Durkheim states, 'is every way of acting, fixed or not, capable of exercising on the individual an external constraint' (ibid., p. 13). Again, the moral aspect of social facts appears to be primary. Durkheim does not discuss the collective conscience as such in the *Rules*, and indeed is no longer concerned with a *single* moral code; the social facts he has in mind are, for example, languages, systems of currency, practices, and any 'ways of acting, thinking, and feeling that present the noteworthy property of existing outside the individual consciousness' (p. 2). This, of course, is in keeping with the view in his first book, *The division of labour in society*, that the collective conscience only exists fully in a totally undifferentiated society, for here, in the case of modern societies, he only discusses diverse social facts. Yet in the *Rules* he makes such statements as 'the collective being . . . is itself a being in its own right' (p. 124), and 'individual minds, forming groups by mingling and fusing, give birth to a being, psychological if you will, but constituting a psychic individuality of a new sort' (p. 103), statements which have often been used against him to prove that his view of society as a reality *sui generis* was more than a methodological precept, but was rather an ontological statement. In either case, the definition of the *conscience collective* provided in *The division of labour in society* is not really elaborated or improved in this methodological essay, although we can now see that social facts are not necessarily ethical in nature, since Durkheim mentions language, for example, as a social fact.

Durkheim's later work on religion is contained in the monograph, *Primitive classification*, which he wrote with M. Mauss, and the book *Elementary forms of religious life*. In the latter, particularly, missing links in the theory of the *conscience collective* are provided (although, as Parsons shows, there is also a basic epistemological shift in Durkheim's position here). By introducing the concept 'collective representations', Durkheim both allows for social facts which are *not* the whole of the *conscience collective*, and admits *non*-moral social facts. His main task in this work is to show that the categories of thought themselves are collective representations (and thus social in origin). By 'representations', Durkheim means the data and concepts reflecting the external world—images and categories, learned in the socialisation process, through which we experience the world (see Wolff 1960, p. 81). Collective representations are those concerning the social environment, as well as those originating *in* it (Durkheim 1915, Conclusion; Parsons 1949, p. 360). For example, since our language and our system of concepts are the product of collective elaboration, the ideas contained in and emerging out of them are collective representations (Durkheim 1915, p. 435). Durkheim's argument is that as the representations (including the categories) *are* collective (or social), they will be found to reflect the structure of the social group. 'They should show the mental states of the group; they should depend upon the way in which this is founded and organized, upon its morphology, upon its religious, moral and economic institutions, etc.' (ibid., p. 16). In particular, religious representations are also collective representations, and similarly reflect social organisations. Again, Durkheim stresses that collective representations are independent of any individual mind (ibid., p. 435).

In the transition from the collective conscience to collective representations, Durkheim changes the meaning of 'conscience' (ambiguous in the original French) from the English 'conscience' to 'consciousness' (see Parsons 1949, p. 359). The representations which make up the *conscience collective* are no longer primarily normative, since the concepts and categories of thought are not *moral* representations. The collective conscience (or consciousness) may now be defined as a sum of collective representations—that is, of concepts and images both reflecting and originating in the social environment, and held in common by the members of a society. Alternatively, as Durkheim is not clear about the relation of the two terms, the *conscience collective* may be that limited number of representations which make up the moral code of a society; that is, conscience, rather than the whole of consciousness. (In the latter interpretation, the distinction is more or less equivalent to Parsons's distinction of value-systems and their wider framework of cultural systems as a whole.) Despite the ambiguity of phrase, and despite the fact that a theory of collective representations and consciousness is nowhere properly worked out by Durkheim, there are here suggestive elements for such a theory. For the first time, it could be seen how sociology can discuss psychic facts which are not only psychological but in an important sense supra-individual. If there *do* exist collective representations, and a total collective conscience or consciousness, independently of their manifestations in the individual members of a society, sociology need neither abandon its 'subjectivist' verstehende approach for what Parsons calls 'radical positivism', nor reduce itself to social psychology. This insight of Durkheim's was one of the most crucial discoveries in the history of sociological theory. Furthermore, it is the basis for a phenomenological sociology which is not only phenomenological but also truly sociological. It is on the Durkheimian conception of collective mental data that this book must ultimately depend.

Nevertheless, as well as failing to elaborate his concept fully,

Durkheim was clearly wrong in his understanding of some aspects of the nature of the *conscience collective*. Most importantly, although Parsons claims that Durkheim was well aware that society only exists as the synthetic product of the association of individuals (Parsons 1949, p. 368), it is apparent that this was not the case in many of Durkheim's insistent statements on the autonomy of social facts. In one place, he explicitly says that the origins of social phenomena cannot be individuals because they exert pressure *on* the latter (Durkheim 1938, pp. 101–2). For those familiar with the later, dialectical analyses of Berger and Luckmann, and Parsons himself, this is of course both a *non sequitur* and false. Again, Durkheim argues: 'Neither Hobbes nor Rousseau seems to have realized how contradictory it is to admit that the individual is himself the author of a machine which has for its essential role his domination and constraint' (1938, p. 122). This ahistorical view of the relation between individual and society goes too far in attempting to demonstrate the reality *sui generis* of social facts and their contemporary autonomy from social interaction. Having pointed out the inadequacies of Durkheim's view, I now want to turn to its more thoroughly worked out exposition in the work of Parsons.

iv Parsons

Parsons's discussion and critique of Durkheim is to be found in his first important book, *The structure of social action*, although in the 1968 introduction to this book, he himself suggests that it is the two works of his second phase—*The social system* and *Towards a general theory of action*—which are more Durkheimian than Weberian. The first book, based on the contributions of Pareto, Durkheim and Weber to sociological theory, develops an approach which owes more to Weber than to either of the others. Social facts, value-systems, etc. are certainly a part of his schema. Indeed, he says, quite early in his book (1949, p. 74),

> it is hoped, in transcending the positivist-idealist dilemma, to show a way of transcending also the old individualism-social organism or, as it is often called, social nominalism-realism dilemma which has plagued social theory to little purpose for so long.

The focus, however, is on the unit act—on the structure of social action. 'The primary basis in this study will be the schema of action, with concrete individuals thought of as adapting means to ends' (1949, p. 30). In other words, in the language of *The social system*, the accent is not on the social system or the cultural system, or even on the personality system as such, but rather on the individual in the process of *acting*, reference to these three systems being relevant but incidental to this. This is Parsons's 'voluntaristic theory of action', which, he claims, is implicit in all three authors he reviews. (He also adds, incidentally, that 'the action frame of reference may be said to have what many, following Husserl, have called, a "phenomenological" status' (p. 733).) It is the later two works which are more relevant to our own investigation, but *The structure of social action* is important for two reasons in this context. In the first place, Parsons's understanding, evaluation and critique of Durkheim are developed here at great length, from which, although we need not accept every aspect of his interpretation, we can see how Parsons takes as his starting point many of Durkheim's theoretical pronouncements. Second, this early work is in fact closely related to what follows, for all these writings are united in the action frame of reference, the difference being in the increasing emphasis on social systems within this framework.

An important point which Parsons makes about Durkheim is the latter's belated recognition of the internalisation of values. The type of constraint exercised by the collective conscience in *The division of labour*, although normative, appears to be *external* in nature. Only later does Durkheim perceive the internal nature of moral constraint (Parsons 1949, pp. 382–3). That is, conformity with the moral code is motivated not only by avoidance of sanctions; the *subjective* character of norms is recognised. This realisation, according to Parsons, also marks the point of Durkheim's final abandonment of positivism for a new version of idealism, where society consists *exclusively* of ideas and sentiments—that is, solely in the minds of individuals (1949, pp. 442—4). Parsons is here referring to *The elementary forms of religious life*. In view of the quotations from Durkheim's other work (above), the observation is remarkable. I do not feel that the evidence is as clear-cut as Parsons makes out, for although it is true that Durkheim abandons his objectivist bias, adopting more of a verstehende position which accepts the subjective element in moral constraint, he nowhere repudiates his earlier firm belief in the autonomy of social facts. Indeed, the resolution of this belief with his new discovery would have been the first step in his perceiving the dialectical nature of the relation between society and the individual.

Parsons's other criticisms are minor, and are mainly concerned with Durkheim's failure to follow up his early leanings towards a voluntaristic theory of action, and his concentration on society as such (a practice which Parsons himself follows to some extent, as we have seen). On the whole, the positive side of Durkheim's influence on Parsons must be stressed, in particular the introduction of the concept of the social fact, and the understanding of the internalisation of norms. With this in mind, we shall consider Parsons's original conception of the social system, and in particular those elements of systems of action which form the mind or consciousness of a society or social group.

I shall have to take for granted an acquaintance with the Parsonian model, since it is impossible to describe briefly a system which takes Parsons himself more than five hundred pages to elaborate. Its essential features are the three configurations, within the general theory of action, of personality, social system and culture. These are interrelated in complex ways, through roles, institutions and the socialisation process. They are further differentiated by the three modes of orientation (cognitive, cathectic and evaluative), so that the cultural system, for example, consists of systems of ideas and beliefs (cognitive primacy), expressive symbols (cathectic primacy) and systems of value orientations (evaluative primacy). Through socialisation, culture patterns are internalised into the individual personality. The orientation of action (and, indirectly, the analysis of the social system) is further differentiated by the five sets of pattern-variables, each offering alternatives of motivation. Non-internalised culture patterns remain as possible objects of orientation in action. The social system itself is related to personality and cultural system as follows (Parsons 1951, pp. 5–6):

> Reduced to the simplest possible terms . . . a social system consists in a plurality of individual actors interacting with each other in a situation which has at least a physical or environmental aspect, actors who are motivated in terms of a tendency to the 'optimization of gratification' and whose relation to their situations, including each other, is defined and mediated in terms of a system of culturally structured and shared symbols.

Its constituents are institutions and their units of status-roles (all differentiated in terms of mode of orientation, and the pattern-variable scheme). Parsons argues that the central concern of sociology should be with the phenomena of institutionalisation (op. cit., p. 548). 'Sociological theory, then, is for us *that aspect of the theory of social systems which is concerned with the phenomena of the institutionalization of patterns of value-orientation in the social system*' (p. 552). It is in the process of institutionalisation that social system, personality, and cultural system meet, for 'institutionalization of cultural patterns means . . . in the integrated sense internalization of the same patterns in the personality' (p. 551).

It should be clear now how Parsons's analysis, making use of the most important of Durkheim's ideas, clarifies them and follows them to their elaborately worked out theoretical conclusions. A comprehension of the socialisation process, through internalisation of cultural patterns and role expectations, and of the parallel process of institutionalisation, on the social level, of roles, patterns of action and values, makes clear the analytical distinction between the three systems of action and their empirical interdependence. It is in this sense that society and social facts, created in the interaction of individuals and subsequently institutionalised, are seen as an external reality confronting the individual, and existing independently of him. (As Berger and Luckmann show, the autonomy of institutions is more than the analytical isolation which Parsons emphasises; the important point about them is that they are now *experienced* as external, objective reality by the individual.) It remains for us to locate in the Parsonian system the collective consciousness which must be our point of reference for a sociology of art. The personality system is clearly irrelevant. Less obviously, it must be stated that neither is the social system, as it is defined in Parsons's scheme, the locus of the social consciousness, for, as we have noted, the social system itself is composed basically of the (institutionalised) patterns of interaction of individual actors (Parsons 1951, p. 5). In *Towards a general theory of action*, the nature of the social system is clearly stated (Parsons 1962, p. 23).

A social system is a system of the interaction of a plurality of persons analyzed within the frame of reference of the theory of action. . . . For most analytical purposes, the most significant unit of social structures is not the person but the role . . . Roles are institutionalized when they are fully congruous with the prevailing culture patterns and are organized around expectations of conformity with morally sanctioned patterns of value-orientation shared by the members of the collectivity in which the role functions.

Although norms, expectations, culture patterns, values, etc. are an integral part of a social system, this is only as they are relevant to its primary focus on role-systems and systems of interaction. It is on the level of cultural systems that ideas, symbols and values exist essentially, and in their own right, and it is on this level of analysis alone that such concepts as 'collective representations', 'total ideology' and 'world-view' belong.

Unlike Durkheim, Parsons carefully differentiates the normative, or moral, aspects of culture from the cognitive and expressive (Parsons 1962, p. 55). The cultural system is constituted by 'the organization of the values, norms, and symbols which guide the choices made by actors and which limit the types of interaction which may occur among actors' (ibid.), either as internalised factors or as objects of orientation. Here Parsons adds that 'if . . . a system of culture is to be manifest in the organization of an empirical action system it must have a certain degree of consistency' (ibid.).

But Parsons always insists on the limited extent of such consistency. 'Very close approximations to complete consistency in the patterns of culture are practically never to be found in large complex social systems' (1962, p. 22). Even within the sub-system of evaluative symbols, he says 'complete consistency of pattern is an ideal type . . . It is indeed probable that complete empirical pattern consistency is impossible' (ibid., p. 172), although maximisation of consistency is defined as one of the functional imperatives of a system. The diversity within empirical value-systems cannot be *a priori* defined out of existence (ibid., p. 176).

> Although a set of *dominant themes* or an *ethos* may be pre-eminent in the concrete value system prevailing in a given society, still there will in addition be many lesser themes representing some or all of the possible pattern-variable combinations to be found in it.

The culture of an existing society, therefore, is not a uniform, totally consistent whole, but rather a heterogeneous combination of variants of the main theme of the ethos (p. 219), located in separate sub-groups of society, for example.

This admission of incomplete pattern consistency is something new in the structural theories we have been considering. Assumption of pattern integration is, of course, a most convenient practice in structural analysis, for then the investigation is rather like fitting together a jigsaw puzzle; only parts seen to have a place in the whole picture need be considered. Where the whole is amorphous, vague of boundary, or containing contradictions, however, the structural analyst might well despair of observing any relevant pieces, or understanding the interrelationships among them. And yet Parsons is right in this observation. Just as Gombrich correctly questions the assumption of cultural unity among cultural historians (see above, chapter 4(i)), Parsons reminds us that pattern-consistency is not given *a priori*. It is on this understanding that we must proceed to locate the collective consciousness (integrated or not) in the cultural system as a whole.

Parsons himself, in his primary interest in the social system, is more concerned with value-orientations than with the other two systems (cognitive and cathectic) of culture (1962, pp. 239–40; see also 1951, p. 349).

> A set of beliefs, of expressive symbols, or of instrumental patterns may be institutionalized in the sense that conformity with the standards in question may become a role-expectation for members of certain collectivities. . . . But only patterns of value-orientation . . . become directly constitutive of the main

structure of alternative types of social relationships which is the central structural focus of social systems. This is the set of primary institutions of a social system. The others are structurally secondary.

I would maintain, however, that the same does not necessarily apply to the sociology of knowledge. Whereas norms are clearly crucial to the understanding of social institutions, with their accompanying expectations, pressures to conform, sanctions, etc. it would be falsely limiting the scope of a sociology of culture to concentrate its attention on value-orientations, to the exclusion of other systems of ideas. In particular, the intimate connection between systems of expressive symbols and works of art and literature should be apparent. Furthermore, the intricacies of the Parsonian model involve the intrusion of evaluative interests into some parts of the other two systems since each system is subdivided twice more, once according to mode of orientation, and once according to its empirical or non-empirical content. For example, in the primarily cognitive belief system, we find, as well as existential beliefs (science, supernatural lore), *evaluative* beliefs, such as ideologies and religious ideas. In systems of expressive symbols, apart from purely expressive symbols, there is evaluative symbolism (e.g. of collective solidarity, or religious symbolism). I cannot claim to understand clearly all the fine distinctions of these categories, and I suspect that a somewhat obsessive concern with the symmetry and closedness of the model leads to some duplication of categories and even to some empty categories. The knowledge which is the concern of the sociology of knowledge is in fact the *whole* of the cultural system, in Parsons's scheme. The study of cultural systems remains part of sociology for two reasons. In the first place, Parsons's analytical model demonstrates the *origin* of these systems in social interaction. (It is possible, however, to take this for granted, in order to concentrate solely on the pure analysis of culture; this, indeed, is the aim of the *Geisteswissenschaften*, such as mathematics, logic, pure aesthetics. See Parsons 1951, p. 554.) Second, the sociology of art, as well as relating artistic creativity to other levels of knowledge (ideology, value-systems, for example), must remain alert to the possibility of perceiving relevant connections between art and the social system itself, unmediated by formal symbol-systems. (It should be noted here that although art, being as it were, one remove from culture symbols in general, in that it may express these symbol-systems themselves, is thus not confined to one category of the cultural system, the same is not necessarily true of *any* branch of knowledge. For example, science clearly does fall into a specific class—that of empirical existential beliefs.)

What, then, in terms of the Parsonian system, is the world-view, or total ideology of a society, and where is it located in the analytical scheme? We have argued that it is to be found essentially in the cultural system (although the latter has its genesis in the social interaction of individual personalities, and although it plays a continuous part empirically in both of the other system-levels). One of the greatest merits of such a detailed model of systems of symbols and ideas is that not only can it help us to answer these questions: it can also be used to show the exact nature, and provide a more precise definition, of such concepts as they are used by the other writers we have considered. For example, it is now far easier to see that Durkheim, in his earlier work, was referring almost exclusively to systems of values, when he talked of the *conscience collective*. Later, he shifted his focus more on to religious, and finally cognitive, systems of beliefs. (The question of where the so-called categories of thought might be fitted into the scheme is another problem. Although they are also often called 'ideas'—e.g. 'innate ideas'—I would probably want to argue that they fall outside the scheme altogether. There is no place for *a priori* knowledge in Parsons's model; furthermore, the categories of thought, in Kantian terminology, *by definition* do not arise in social interaction, unlike the socially based categories of the later Durkheim, and thus are not part of culture.) The 'world vision' of Goldmann is less easy to categorise, and is more diffuse, probably including Parsons's sub-systems of philosophy (non-empirical existential beliefs), ideologies and religious beliefs. Lévi-Strauss's 'innate structuring capacity', like the categories of thought, is outside the scheme, being *a priori*, and not grounded in action and experience. Mannheim's distinction between particular and total ideologies can be seen as the difference between systems of empirical, evaluative beliefs and the much wider world-view comprising expressive and evaluative as well as belief systems. What I think has been learned from the preceding sections of this essay is that it is a mistake to define the concept of a world-view in terms that are too narrow. Having understood, with the help of Parsons's model, the nature and diversity, as well as the relationships, of different forms of knowledge, we must also have realised that there are cognitive, appreciative *and* evaluative elements in a *conscience collective* which is *consciousness*, and not a con*science*. But although I have said that knowledge is coterminous with culture, I do not want to equate the collective consciousness with the cultural system in its entirety. For example, science includes many extremely esoteric statements, whose total irrelevance to everyday life makes it rather ridiculous to call them part of the belief system of the community, even though, because of the institutionalisation of scientific enquiry and the status of any scientific discoveries officially in the social system, such statements are formally part of that body of knowledge. Apart from modifications of this sort, I conclude that the collective consciousness is not to be restricted in definition to any sub-systems of the cultural system. If it is to remain the wider, and more useful, concept intended by Goldmann, Mannheim and others, the relevance of the whole of the cultural system must be admitted.

Unfortunately, this is as far as we can go, in looking at world-views from the point of view of Parsonian theory. There is no formula which can be provided, advising the sociologist actually where to look for a neat and coherent world-view in any empirical society. We cannot now tell him to perform some addition or other computation of, say the chief value-system with the basic scientific beliefs, the average ideological views and the established artistic standards. This is further complicated by the fact that, as we have noted, consistency of pattern cannot be assumed, and is indeed highly improbable. The only positive hint Parsons feels able to give is that there is a certain 'strain to consistency' within total cultural systems (Parsons 1951, p. 350) which, given the difficulties involved for an individual in holding inconsistent views, and the resultant strain, is a fair hypothesis. The diversity of groups and sub-groups within a society must not be overlooked, however. One might even say that it is the *value* of Parsons's analysis that it leaves us in no doubt as to the validity of Gombrich's critique of cultural history with its assumption of unified structures, which it calls world-views.

There are two final points I want to make before turning from the discussion of structural-functionalism to another approach. Both concern certain inadequacies in Parsons's theory from the point of view of the kind of sociology of knowledge, and of art, being developed here. In the first place, the position of the arts in the system is not adequately developed. Art, and the role of the artist, are discussed, but only in the context of the sub-system of expressive symbols, that is, those symbols which are 'that part of the cultural tradition most directly integrated with the cathectic interests of the actor' (Parsons 1951, p. 386). This means, therefore, that art is simply the 'communication of affect'; as Parsons says, expressive symbols are objects of gratification (op. cit., p. 386). But this, as we have argued, is falsely to restrict the nature of the expressive power of such symbols. Furthermore, it is to pre-judge the important issue of whether there is a propaganda, educational or informational aspect of works of art, or whether they are *purely* 'affect'. Thus, it may not only be *specifically* religious symbolism which expresses the solidarity of collectivities (p. 397), for example. A sociology of art must be able to account for *any* of the social facts expressed in art, whether these be acceptance of attitude system, values, strain arising in conflicting roles and values, religion or ideology. This is not possible within the Parsonian scheme, at least as it stands in the works under consideration. The system of expressive (including artistic) symbols is not satisfactorily described. Parsons himself acknowledges as much: 'We have a very well-developed knowledge of the structure of belief systems as such, but a very fragmentary one of the structure of systems of expressive symbols' (1951, p. 427). Art is, in some sense, an expressive system (although, to repeat an important qualification, *what* it expresses is not limited to cathectic interests). Until the nature and language of expression is also understood, our sociology of art is lacking in comprehension.

My final criticism, which I shall here state briefly, is connected with the preceding point, for I believe that its correction would point the way to the solution of the problem just discussed. Again, it concerns the question of meaning. It is true that Parsons's action theory begins with action and interaction, with its subjectivist perspective, and that the subjective features of the social system—expectations, conformity, role, pattern-variables and choice—are central to the model throughout. Nevertheless, and this is particularly true when we reach the level of abstraction of the cultural system, the meanings are not the existential meanings of the individual in society, but formal, generalised abstractions, only loosely based on a Weberian, verstehende analysis. Because the model itself is so carefully thought out, so exactly divided into clear-cut categories, empirical facts, including meanings, are *selectively* observed—that is, only as the model directs our vision. Now meaning, in the phenomenological sense in which we have been using the term, is not a collection of separate, even if genetically connected ideas, symbols and orientations, but is rather a *totality*. This is why, in the end, the Parsonian scheme must be rejected. And in rejecting it in favour of an approach that starts from this totality of meaning, we are re-opening the possibility of talking about the totality and coherence of world-view. What turned out to be impossible in structural-functional sociological terms may prove to be quite legitimate from the perspective of a new kind of theory.

7   Hermeneutic philosophy and the sociology of knowledge

So far, I have avoided any systematic discussion of the problem of method in the social sciences, either simply admitting commitment to one method in preference to another, or merely mentioning traditional and contemporary debates in the area of methodology. In the pages that follow, it will no longer be possible to sidestep these problems, for in hermeneutic theory, subject-matter and method are intrinsically connected. A sociology of knowledge grounded in hermeneutics will be seen to define both its own object and its method of grasping this object. Furthermore, not only is the methodological approach to the subject-matter of sociology and the humanities implied in hermeneutic theory; such theory leads beyond method into its own philosophical conceptions of knowledge itself, and of existence. In other words, method involves, and is involved in, epistemology and ontology. In chapter 3 this overlap of traditional boundaries was discussed in the general context of the sociology of knowledge. Here the radical claim will be re-assessed in the terms of its proponents, and the limits of the philosophical insights of hermeneutic theory, as ontology, pointed out. As a thorough and elaborate exposition of the nature of hermeneutic knowledge, Gadamer's *Wahrheit und Methode* (1965) will be taken to state the case of hermeneutics. Criticisms of Gadamer by other authors will then be examined, and an overall assessment of the advantages and limitations of hermeneutic theory for the sociology of knowledge will be attempted.

Hermeneutics, according to Gadamer, is the confluence point of three important traditions in the cultural sciences (*Geisteswissenschaften*); namely the phenomenology of Husserl, the historicism of Dilthey and the hermeneutic-existential philosophy of Heidegger (1965, p. xxix).

> The scrupulousness of phenomenological description, which Husserl urged on us, the scope of the historical horizon, in

102

which Dilthey placed all philosophising, and not least the penetration of both impulses by the initiative received from Heidegger decades ago, show the framework in which the author has placed himself and under whose obligation he remains in spite of all imperfection of realisation.

Here we may note that one of the most damaging attacks on phenomenological sociology (including ethnomethodology) is the accusation that the historical perspective of social action—dialectical or otherwise, depending on the allegiance of the critic—is ignored completely and that, similarly, the structural context of meaningful action cannot be accommodated in a phenomenological framework. One of the most important claims of hermeneutic theory, then, is the ability to retain the phenomenological intuition, at the same time comprehending the wider perspectives of society and history. The Heideggerian element in Gadamer's thought, despite being the most difficult to grasp, is fundamental. In Heidegger's ontology are found the hermeneutic conceptions of the nature of truth, the relation of knower and known and the method of Verstehen, and the existential structure of being and history (Gadamer 1965, pp. 249–50). For Heidegger, truth *is* historical, for, as Gadamer says, Being itself is Time. This means, not only that the past must be grasped in its historical context, but also, and more radically, that this context *includes* the contemporary interpreter. Verstehen must thus grasp the *totality* of world-experience. '[The concept "hermeneutic"] designates the fundamental movement of *Dasein*, which constitutes its finiteness and historicity, and includes hence the whole of its world-experience' (p. xvi). To put this another way, understanding is also *self*-understanding. Interpretation of the past is always, and necessarily, from the standpoint of the present. But Gadamer is careful to point out that this is not merely to return to the subjectivist theory of intuitive or empathic transposition of the interpreter into the past. 'Understanding itself is not to be thought of so much as an action of subjectivity, as an entering into a tradition, in which past and present continually mediate one another' (pp. 274–5). As he sees (and Dilthey failed to see), this attempt to obliterate the self is doomed to failure (p. 283). The interpreter can only take part in the past with, and by virtue of, his own historicity. As Gadamer puts it, hermeneutics is not a mysterious communion of souls, but the taking part in a common meaning (p. 276). In this light, the notions of truth and objectivity must be re-examined, for it follows that the 'truth' about the past alters with every present. The implications for the sociology of knowledge, with its perennial epistemological problem of the relativity of all thought, are profound. Not only is the dependence of sociological (as of all other) knowledge on social and historical position recognised and admitted: it is regarded as a positive factor in the practice of the cultural sciences. But Gadamer, again following Heidegger, takes the argument even further. Rather than concluding that inevitable relativity makes the notion of truth irrelevant, he argues that historicity *guarantees* the truth of the interpretation. 'What the tool of method does not perform must rather, and can in effect, be performed by a discipline of question and enquiry, which guarantees truth' (p. 465; see also pp. xxv ff.). Before returning to a defence of the scientific method, and the traditional concept of objectivity, as a critic of Gadamer might immediately be inclined to do, one must understand that the 'truth' of which he is speaking is nothing to do with, and is not in competition with, the truth of scientific method. 'The *Geisteswissenschaften* move closer to modes of experience which lie outside science ... modes of experience in which truth comes to light, truth which cannot be verified by the methodology of science' (p. xxvi). The hermeneutic method of Verstehen has as its task the discovery of a truth not attainable by science. From the point of view of the *Geisteswissenschaften*, the scientific search for an ahistorical object-in-itself is misconceived, for there *is* no such object. ('Ein solcher Gegenstand an sich existiert offenbar überhaupt nicht' (p. 269).) There can be no world without *Daseins*-relativity. 'Neither the biological nor the physical universe can in truth deny the *Daseins*-relativity which affects it' (p. 428).

This brings Gadamer to the question of prejudices (*Vorurteile*).[1] Traditionally, at least in Anglo-American social science, the intrusion of the investigator's personal prejudices, assumptions and preferences into his research and observation is regarded as the paramount crime against the canons of objectivity. His aim must be to rid himself of *all* preconceptions, in order to approach his material with an open mind, without directing his enquiry towards certain data while failing to perceive other equally relevant data. The respectful awe in which objectivity, thus defined, is held, is not confined to the radical positivists of the social sciences. Even Weber, who devoted so much energy to making respectable the method of Verstehen in the face of neo-Kantian orthodoxy, was at pains to stress the value-free procedure necessary for objectivity (see chapter 3(i)). As might be expected, Gadamer turns the problem completely around. He condemns the rise of this discrediting of prejudice which began with the Enlightenment and which almost has the power of a religious belief

---

[1] *Vorurteil* literally means 'bias' or 'prejudice' (*urteilen*: to judge). It is clearly not used here in its strongest (and derogatory) sense of a blind, distorted or mistaken belief which, almost by definition, is false, but rather in the weaker sense of a preconception (a pre-judgment), which does indeed direct and even distort perception, but which is all the same neither inimical to the truth nor immune to correction and adjustment.

by now. 'This fundamental prejudice of the Enlightenment is the prejudice against prejudices in general, and thereby the overthrow of tradition' (p. 255). In the first place, prejudices are an unavoidable attribute of human existence, or, as he puts it, they are the historical reality of being of an individual. ('Die Vorurteile [sind] des einzelnen weit mehr als seine Urteile die geschichtliche Wirklichkeit seines Seins' (p. 261).) This much is also recognised by Habermas, in his *Knowledge and Human Interests*, and his earlier article, 'Knowledge and interest' (1966), where he argues that objectivism is an illusion, attempting to show the origin of cognition in interests deriving primarily from work, language and authority. Indeed, even some sociologists in England and America are prepared to go further than Weber and Mannheim in admitting the value-relevance of any (social) scientific enquiry (see, for example, Gouldner 1971). But what Gadamer proceeds to argue is that prejudices (at least, *legitimate* prejudices; pp. 261 ff.) are necessary conditions for understanding. The historical consciousness, seeing its own present, thus brings prejudices into play in Verstehen, which is seen as a fusion of horizons of past and present. 'There is no horizon of the present for itself, any more than there are historical horizons which one has to acquire. *Rather, Verstehen is always the process of the merging of such horizons, supposedly existing for themselves*' (p. 289).

Here we come across the conception of the hermeneutic circle, in one of its senses (for, as far as I can see, Gadamer uses the phrase in at least two ways) (pp. 250 ff.). The circular procedure works as follows: we approach our material with certain prejudices, or anticipations, originating in our own historicity. At the same time, we must retain a certain 'openness' (pp. 253 and 344) to our object (whether this be a text or anything else). This receptiveness to the 'otherness' of the material, allowing it to speak for itself, creates a balance (or a dialectic) between prejudice and openness. By *controlling* our anticipations, we are enabled to *revise* them, since our openness to the subject-matter allows distorting prejudices to be discovered. 'Verstehen of what is there consists in the working out of a . . . projection (*Vorentwurf*), which is certainly constantly revised by what results from further penetration into the meaning' (p. 251). A new definition of objectivity is thus arrived at—namely, the verification a prejudice finds in its working out. ('Die Bewährung, die eine Vormeinung durch ihre Ausarbeitung findet' (p. 252).) But here again, it is important to make it clear, to avoid misguided criticisms, that Gadamer *is* redefining 'objectivity'; the object thus arrived at is still not the object-in-itself of the sciences, or even an approximation to it. Its truth is still historical, relative and socially determined.

The circularity of the hermeneutic method, then, lies partly in its

105

controlled oscillations between present and past horizons, and the movement from one to the other, and round again back to the starting point of the first. It also lies in the simultaneous movement between whole and part (p. 275; p. xxi). That is, understanding the single aspects of a society—particular acts, a certain text, a painting—presupposes a prior knowledge of the total context (the society, its whole culture and tradition). This, in turn, however, can only be grasped through its specific manifestations. What seems an insuperable paradox to non-dialectical thinkers is resolved by Gadamer's description of the continual circular movement, mediating between whole (anticipated in the sense mentioned above) and part. The process, according to Gadamer, is of a conversational nature, involving a continual checking and re-checking (p. 349). Obviously, the question of the role of prejudice is related to this secondary notion of the hermeneutic circle too, for the interpreter returns from his observation of the facts to modify his preconception of the whole, a preconception which is essential, since only what has a completed unity of sense can be understood. ('Nur das verständlich ist, was wirklich eine vollkommene Einheit von Sinn darstellt' (p. 278).) What prevents our prejudices and anticipations being totally erroneous and misleading is the vital fact of our belonging to the same universal tradition as those we are studying. The horizon of the interpreter is determining as a *possibility*, which helps him to appropriate his historical material (p. 336).

> To that extent, the interpreter's own horizon is determining, but even that is not as a particular standpoint which one holds or enforces, but more like an opinion and a possibility, which one brings into play and puts at stake, and which contributes to appropriating truthfully what is said in the text.

Gadamer makes the statement that the circle is ontological rather than methodological. ('Der Zirkel des Verstehens, ist also überhaupt nicht ein "methodischer" Zirkel, sondern beschreibt ein ontologisches Strukturmoment des Verstehens' (p. 277).) Although I am not altogether confident that I understand his meaning here (for surely the hermeneutic procedure he has just described *is* also the method followed by the investigator?), I take it that what he is emphasising is the *ontological foundation* of such a method. In other words, the hermeneutic circle is not simply a heuristic, methodological device, invented to facilitate the approach to historico-cultural material; it is the reality of being of interpreter and interpreted, and their mediation and unity in the history of events.

The hermeneutic re-definition of Verstehen, depending as it does on a philosophy which is alien to those trained in the logic and empiricism of the scientific method, is difficult to comprehend in its own terms. Perhaps the notion which best crystallises the idea of history, the nature of knowledge, the conception of culture and tradition, and the role of the sociologist or historian in Gadamer's thought is that of the *wirkungsgeschichtliche Bewusstsein* (pp. 284 ff.). Literally, this is the 'effect-historical consciousness'; it refers to the consciousness of the historian or sociologist and contains in the single complex predicate all the essential elements of hermeneutic theory outlined in the preceding paragraphs. The interpreter must recognise both his subject's and his own place in history, in the tradition of real events, *and* must comprehend the relationship and fusion of the two standpoints in his work. This, briefly, is what is meant by the insistence that understanding is *wirkungsgeschichtlich*. ('Verstehen is by its nature an effect-historical operation' (p. 283).) The exercise of the *wirkungsgeschichtliche Bewusstsein*, in Verstehen, is in effect a fusion of the horizons of present and past (p. 289). As Gadamer puts it in another passage, the historical consciousness must think with its own historicity. ('Das historische Bewusstsein . . . muss in Wahrheit die eigene Geschichtlichkeit mitdenken' (p. 343).) At the same time, the *wirkungsgeschichtliche Bewusstsein* must *retain* the distance between present and past, acknowledging the 'otherness' of the other and of the past, as the Verstehen of the Thou (pp. 340 ff.). (This may be compared with Schutz's phenomenological analysis of the experience of the Thou and the We, in *The phenomenology of the social world*.) The mode of completion of the *wirkungsgeschichtliche Bewusstsein* consists in the mixing of horizons of understanding mediating between the text and the interpreter (p. 359).

It should be clear by now how hermeneutic Verstehen differs radically both from Dilthey's empathic but ahistorical transference, and from the Weberian notion of a more objective kind of understanding of meanings (in terms of ideal types of rationality, for example), with its typically obsessive emphasis on subsequent scientific verification. Furthermore, it goes beyond a pure phenomenology of inter-personal or cross-cultural understanding, existential or otherwise, for it allows the mind to see itself *in* a context, rather than bracketing off any world or context perceived other than *through* the mind. The emphasis is still on the consciousness of the interpreter; where phenomenology would take this as the epistemological frame of reference, in terms of which alone both past and present are mediated (and thus whose objectivity is relative to the single observer), hermeneutic philosophy forces the interpreter to begin by grasping the place of his own consciousness in its historico-cultural context. Here, indeed, is a possible response to the critique of Paul Ricoeur (chapter 5(i)), who objected that, just as structuralism ignores the meaningful content of action, phenomenology loses the perspective of supra-personal phenomena. The *wirkungsgeschichtliche*

Bewusstsein, by its very nature, is able to take account of both. Such a brief summary and interpretation of a five hundred page book clearly does not do justice to an extremely complex and detailed work. Nevertheless, it was my intention to expound Gadamer's theory in order to proceed to investigate its usefulness in solving some of the problems we have come across in the sociology of world-views, and their expression in art, and not primarily to transmit another's work to a wider audience. There are, therefore, important omissions of detail in the preceding exposition, including a number of apparent contradictions in Gadamer's text. One case of this, which perhaps ought to be mentioned, if not resolved, at this point, concerns the question of absolute, or ahistorical, truth. As we have seen, Gadamer argues that there is no point of view outside history ('einen Standort ausserhalb der Geschichte . . . gibt es in Wahrheit nicht' (p. 357)), and that the best the sociologist can do is to work with full consciousness of his own historicity and relativity. The implication is that truth varies from generation to generation, as each age will comprehend in a different way a past age. Gadamer explicitly states that a text, for example, presents different aspects to different times, and that, indeed, there *is* no object in itself (p. 269). However, he also says that the hermeneutic fusion of horizons leads to an overall *single* horizon, in which human life always lives. He talks of this as an 'elevation to a higher generality', above one's own and the other's particularity: ('Die Erhebung zu einer höheren Allgemeinheit, die nicht nur die eigene Particularität, sondern auch die des anderen überwindet' (p. 288)). He also talks of the 'hermeneutic universal'. Of course, the eccentric use of the concepts of 'truth' and 'objectivity' help to compound the apparent discrepancy. At times, it sounds rather as if Gadamer holds a view of truth and an ontology similar to Scheler's, which posits a realm of *ideal* essences, which can only be more or less approximately grasped by men at different periods, bound as they are by the relativity of the *real* factors of their existence. Gadamer, however, makes it clear that absolute knowledge can *never* be attained. On the whole, the evidence is too slight to attribute to him with any certainty an ontological theory of Platonic ideality. I think we must take it that his references to objectivity, truth and a higher generality, etc. always imply historical relativity. (Towards the end of his book, however, as I shall show later, he appears more unambiguously committed to a certain ontological idealism.)

This exposition of hermeneutic theory, the exercise of the *wirkungsgeschichtliche Bewusstsein*, and the hermeneutic circle, is in fact only the central section of a three-part book. I want to place it now in the context of the whole work, for two reasons. First, Gadamer's progression of argument both suggests the need for such a method, and demonstrates it in practice. Second, the first and last sections deal with, respectively, aesthetics and language, both of which are primary concerns of this book, and both of which recur even in the more general discussion of a sociology of knowledge. I shall follow my account of Gadamer's theory of art and language with a new attempt to approach the theoretical problems of the sociology of art and literature and of related forms of knowledge.

Gadamer approaches hermeneutic theory through aesthetics because, in his view, the experience of art is ideally suited to demonstrate the limits of the scientific consciousness in the cultural sciences (Introduction, p. xxvi). His intention is to use a critique of aesthetic consciousness to develop a concept of knowledge and truth which corresponds to the whole of our hermeneutic experience. The section is thus entitled 'Exposition of the problem of truth in the experience of art' ('Freilegung der Wahrheitsfrage an der Erfahrung der Kunst'). Its target is the traditional concept of aesthetic experience as a pure and timeless communion of the observer with the work of art. For one thing, a painting, for example, may represent an allegory (this being particularly true of pre-Baroque art; pp. 68 ff.); *Erlebnis-kunst*-theory[1] would dismiss this aspect as irrelevant, at least to aesthetic considerations. Gadamer argues that it is an integral part of the painting, *as* a work of art. But even in the case of less explicitly documentary art, aesthetic abstraction is wrong. The work loses its place and its world through the process of aesthetic differentiation, and this loss is disastrous. 'Through the "aesthetic distinction" (*ästhetische Unterscheidung*) the work loses its place and the world to which it belongs, as it comes to belong to the aesthetic consciousness' (p. 83). The aesthetic dimension must be transcended, argues Gadamer, for the *true* experience of art (p. 92) involves the understanding of meaning. (Indeed, this is not merely a precept to be followed, but necessarily true, since perception itself always includes meaning: 'Wahrnehmung erfasst immer Bedeutung' (p. 87).) Thus the real aesthetic experience is the act of a historical spirit, not a timeless presence. 'The pantheon of art is not a timeless presence, presenting itself to the pure aesthetic consciousness, but the act of a historical spirit, gathering and assembling itself' (p. 92). For, Gadamer adds, world-view is the truth, visible in art (p. 93).

Gadamer's principal example here is visual art, but he intends his comments to apply to all the arts. He does deal briefly with literature

---

[1] The theory that art originates in experience, and is the expression of that experience, and which has come to mean also, that art is aimed *at* aesthetic experience. Gadamer argues that the dual aspects of the theory are connected (p. 66). He traces the theory to Goethe and his contemporaries.

in a later section, arguing that the written work as well as the painted work can only be grasped via its ontology, and not simply in a pure aesthetic reading. ('Nur von der Ontologie des Kunstwerks her . . . lässt sich also die Kunstart der Literatur begreifen' (p. 153).) That is, the object of enquiry is not to be the aesthetic consciousness, but rather the mode of being (*Seinsweise*) of the work of art (p. 96). (He adds that literature, unlike other relics of past life, is 'pure Geist', and thus, presumably, particularly amenable to hermeneutic comprehension: 'Nothing is so pure a trace of spirit as writing' (p. 156).) This means not merely that interpretation involves historical understanding, but also that it takes into account the nature of artistic creativity and representation itself; this appears to be what Gadamer means when he says that a work must be approached via its ontology, and this, of course, is to extend considerably the scope of aesthetic understanding. In outlining the ontology of art for us, Gadamer begins with the analogy of *play* (*Spiel*), which he describes as 'movement without aim or effort' ('ohne Zweck und Absicht, ohne Anstrengung' (pp. 100–1)), whose rules make it master of the player. The player faces the game as a reality—as a closed world not dependent on his subjectivity. Similarly, he argues, art has its autonomous nature. Inasmuch as a work of art itself is play, its being is inseparable from its representation (p. 116). Thus, however much it is changed in the representation, it remains itself. This is what Gadamer calls the 'contemporaneity of art' (*Gleichzeitigkeit* (p. 121), which is *not* the same thing as the simultaneity of aesthetic consciousness). The point is that the presentation of the work, however far from its origin, wins full presence; its existence is only in *becoming*. (He gives the example of a festival, which occurs annually, but is not thereby reduced to mere repetition.)

If I have followed Gadamer's rather difficult argument correctly, it can now be summarised as follows. In the case of works of art, we have, first, to take into account their ontology—the nature of artistic creativity itself, which, Gadamer explains, is analogous to that of play in its independence of the artist/player. But this autonomous existence is nevertheless dependent on (and interdependent with) the actual representation of any work/game, and the latter, being essentially historical, necessitates the hermeneutic task of *Daseins*-analysis: that is, the work must be grasped in its own historicity. Finally, the historicity of the *present* also comes into play in the interpretation of art, for the hermeneutic understanding is neither re-creation of the past nor the more intuitive exercise of the historical consciousness (p. 158) but involves the mediation of past and present (i.e. the contemporaneity of history). Works of art are at the same time contemporary with every present, *and* placed in their historical origin and function (p. 115).

That works originate in a past, from which they project into the present as lasting monuments, makes their existence far from an object of aesthetic or historical consciousness. As long as they stand in their functions, they are contemporary with every present.

At this point, I want to mention one critical attack on Gadamer, because the writer is concerned solely with the part of Gadamer's work which we have just considered, namely his aesthetic theory, conceding that the rest of Gadamer's book is better able to withstand critical analysis. In an article entitled 'The questionability of transcending the aesthetic dimension of art' ('Die Fragwürdigkeit der Transzendierung der ästhetischen Dimension der Kunst'), Oskar Becker proposes to re-instate the pure aesthetic consciousness. He defends the Platonic abstraction which ignores as irrelevant the historical situation of artist, work of art and contemporary interpreter. He reminds us that Gadamer, following Heidegger's *Existenzphilosophie*, states the paramount importance of the life-historical context and of turning the discontinuity of aesthetic experience into the continuity of our own *Dasein*. Becker is totally opposed to this contamination of the pure aesthetic experience. In a higher life, he insists, visionary moments break through historical existence. ('Jedoch liesse sich durchaus ein hohes Leben denken, in dem visionäre Augenblicke die historische Existenz durchbrechen' (Becker 1962, p. 232).) While he is prepared to admit that there can be, for example, religious meanings in a painting, he argues that these are separate and separable from its *aesthetic* meanings (pp. 235–6).

It would be as well to note critically here that for example the religious and the artistic significance of a work can very well be separated. . . . The unity of the religious or political-ideological significance and the artistic 'statement' is by no means self-evident or a priori necessary.

Not all understanding is, as Gadamer thinks, a form of self-understanding. There is a form of pure appreciation of art, which involves less of self and ignores historical context. In other words, the transcending of the aesthetic dimension is both unnecessary and mistaken. 'It appears . . . that the aesthetic dimension cannot legitimately be transcended' (p. 236). Becker concludes, not that hermeneutics is the wrong method for the social and cultural sciences, but that art is a particularly bad example to choose to illustrate the need for hermeneutic understanding in the *Geisteswissenschaften*.

In a sense, Becker is of course right. Clearly there *is* such a thing as a purely aesthetic appreciation of a work of art, detached from historical considerations. But there are two points to be made here. The first is made by Gadamer himself, in the Foreword to the second edition of the book (p. XVI). He grants that the aesthetic quality of a work of art rests on rules of construction and a level of formation which in the end transcend all limits of historical origin and cultural membership, but raises the question of how much taste in or knowledge of works of art is *only* formally developed, rather than (historically) formed. This, I think, is a valid question, and Becker's assumption of the *a priori* nature of aesthetic judgment is no more convincing than the empiricist view that such judgment originates in experience, tradition and other forms of life than the aesthetic, whether or not its contemporary exercise appears in total abstraction from historical data. The second point goes further in undermining Becker's criticisms. Granted that there *is* such a thing as the pure, ahistorical, aesthetic consciousness, and that therefore there is, in one sense, no reason or need to transcend the aesthetic dimension in order to achieve the 'higher moments' of aesthetic experience, this in no way damages Gadamer's own case. Indeed, he acknowledges the aesthetic dimension, and devotes a lengthy discussion to its exposition, before proceeding to argue in favour of its hermeneutic extension. His thesis is that in transcending pure aesthetics we attain a more comprehensive understanding and appreciation of works of art, *without* relinquishing the aesthetic element. It is in this way that the inner coherence of the aesthetic and the historical moment in the consciousness of a culture can be perceived (p. 82). This he calls the *real* experience of art, in contrast to the arbitrary abstraction of pure aesthetics (p. 92).

> If this aesthetic abstraction is subsequently understood as to the contents, however, and transformed into the demand to understand art 'purely aesthetically', we see now how this demand for abstraction to the true experience of art gets into an insoluble contradiction.

If Gadamer's theory of art is to be attacked, it cannot be on the grounds that a narrower concept of the meaning and experience of art can also be demonstrated, and this is all that Becker has done. If it is true that one may appreciate a painting without understanding all its religious, mythological, allegorical or symbolic references, it is also true that this additional knowledge permits a broader view, and thus appreciation, of the work, which at the same time includes the aesthetic element. (To say this is not, it should by now be clear, to detract from the pure philosophy of art as a discipline, for clearly it still makes sense to enquire into the nature of the aesthetic judgment.) For the moment, then, we shall accept Gadamer's account of the hermeneutic comprehension of art and literature, and postpone other possible criticisms until we have considered the rest of his book.

As I showed earlier in this chapter, Gadamer goes on to extend the hermeneutic method to all the cultural sciences. Strictly speaking, we ought not to call it the 'hermeneutic method', as Gadamer points out in several places that hermeneutics is not so much a method as a 'discipline which guarantees truth' (p. 465). (Hence the title of the book, and the recurring stress on the distinction between truth and method.) Nevertheless, Gadamer does at times talk about the method (e.g. 'As one can see, the problem of method is completely determined by its object' (p. 297)), and I cannot see that hermeneutics is anything other than a practice for the cultural sciences. I think Gadamer's emphatic distinction really means that he wants to make it clear that his theory is not *merely* a methodology for the *Geisteswissenschaften*, but is in fact a complete *ontology*, with its derivative epistemology and methodology implied. Indeed, I shall argue later that it is *only* as a methodology that hermeneutics can be evaluated for sociology, and, further, that it is precisely in his excursion into ontology and metaphysics that Gadamer abandons the critical attitude which, I would maintain, is imperative for any empirical discipline, for the social as much as for the natural sciences.

The critical analysis of, first, the aesthetic consciousness, and then the nature of the cultural–historical sciences in general, in revealing the limits of the scientific consciousness (p. XXVI; see above) offers a new theory/method which, based on the hermeneutic-existential philosophy of life and being itself, unites the cultural sciences with the whole of our world-experience. 'The following enquiries . . . attempt . . . to develop a concept of knowledge and of truth corresponding to the whole of our hermeneutic experience' (Introduction, p. XXVII). The historical dimension permits the joining of horizons necessary for the understanding of the actions, institutions and cultural manifestations of an earlier age. The mode of completion of the *wirkungsgeschichtliche Bewusstsein*, according to Gadamer, is the uniting of horizons of Verstehen mediating between the text (for example) and the interpreter. ('Seine Vollzugsweise beschrieben wir als die Verschmelzung der Horizonte des Verstehens, die zwischen Text und Interpreten vermittelt' (p. 359).) In the third and final section of the book, Gadamer considers the relevance of *language*, which, he submits, is central to the method of Verstehen. The dialogue between interpreter and his subjects can only take place *through* language. 'The mingling of horizons which occurs in Verstehen (is) the particular achievement of language' (p. 359). As he puts it, the process of Verstehen is linguistic; speech is the medium in which the understanding of one's partner, or of other things, is

113

accomplished. ('Die Sprache ist die Mitte, in der sich die Verständigung der Partner und das Einverständnis über die Sache vollzieht' (p. 361).) Language is the universal medium in which Verstehen is completed. This can also be stated by saying that language is the concretion of the *wirkungsgeschichtliche Bewusstsein*. ('Die Sprachlichkeit des Verstehens ist *die Konkretion des wirkungsgeschichtlichen Bewusstseins*' (p. 367).)

The importance of language does not only lie in the linguistic nature of the hermeneutic dialogue, however, but derives from an even more fundamental aspect of human existence; namely, the inescapable linguistic element in the primary experience. Gadamer here fully endorses the Humboldtian theory of linguistic relativity (see chapter 2(ii)). The language-view of man, he maintains, *is* his world-view ('Sprachansicht als Weltansicht' (p. 419)); the *Dasein* of the world is only grasped linguistically by man. Therefore, there is no position *outside* the world of language. ('Es gibt keinen Standort ausserhalb der sprachlichen Welterfahrung' (p. 429).) Nevertheless, this is not to say that the world as perceived is the arbitrary creation of a linguistic form. Gadamer appears to believe that, although we cannot reach it *except* through language, there *is* a world independent of language in some sense, for he says that the world *presents itself* in language, but is *not* its object (p. 426).

> In language, the world presents itself. The linguistic world-experience is 'absolute'. It surmounts all relativities of being, because it grasps all being-in-itself, in whichever relations (relativities) it appears. The linguisticness of our world-experience is prior to everything that is perceived and considered as existing. *The fundamental reference of language and world does not signify that the world becomes the object of language.*

(Cf. here the theory of Dufrenne, discussed earlier, p. 62.) In this case, his often repeated statement that there is no world-in-itself, without *Daseins*-relativity (p. 428) would have to be taken to mean that there *can* be no world for any human being without the perspective of his *Daseins*-relativity. Again, I am not sure whether Gadamer does here imply the existence of the Platonic, ideal world of the noumena. It is not important to determine this point, though; what *is* important, and is indubitably the case, is that he believes in the insuperable perspectivism of any one human being.

The possibility of moving between language-worlds, which proved so problematic for other subscribers to the theory of relativity, is easily dealt with by Gadamer. First, and in line with his general views on hermeneutic understanding, there is no question of abandoning one's own linguistic perspective in order to enter that of the subject. The interpreter necessarily maintains his *own* language.

Equating the translator with the interpreter, Gadamer says: 'The translator [must] maintain the right of his own native language, into which he is translating, and yet allow the foreign-ness, even the hostile-ness of the text and its expression, to stand for itself' (p. 364). From the perspective of our own world, we can enter other language-worlds (without, however, imposing on them our own categories), and return to our own world with new experiences. ('Als Reisende kehren wir mit neuen Erfahrungen heim' (p. 424).) It is possible thus, says Gadamer, to raise oneself above one's *Umwelt*, without leaving it (p. 421). In overcoming our prejudices and limits by entering other language-worlds, we *do not* thus abandon our own. 'If we overcome the prejudices and limitations of our hitherto existing world-experience, by entering foreign language-worlds, that does not mean that we abandon and negate our own world' (p. 424).

Clearly, this is simply an extension of Gadamer's general theory of cultural understanding; that is, the historian/social scientist/interpreter starts within his own existentially-defined situation, which itself leads him to formulate the questions he will pose and to postulate or anticipate a meaning for his material. This will be done, however, with an openness which comes from a consciousness of these prejudices, and so will allow him to perceive the data in the context of their own historicity and thereby adjust and correct his anticipations. The material, whether this be a painting or any other cultural object, is not and cannot be understood exactly as it would be by its creator or his contemporaries. (Indeed, with regard to language-understanding at least, Gadamer even admits that certain overtones of the original are bound to be lacking in a later interpretation. 'Every translation which takes its task seriously, is plainer and shallower than the original. Even if it is a masterly reproduction, it must lack some of the overtones that resonate in the original' (p. 364).) Despite this reservation, Gadamer is in no doubt that the understanding of the past is not, in the derogatory sense, merely ideological. Because of the interpreter's openness to his material, and because of the common tradition, or hermeneutic universal, in which he is united *with* it, his own *Daseins*-relativity will only marginally distort, but not totally define, his reading of the past. The recognition of the linguisticness of human experience, according to Gadamer, gives the analysis of hermeneutic experience a broader horizon (p. 423), in the sense that the grasp of the language-world amounts to a grasp of the world of experience.

Does this lead to the conclusion that hermeneutics is simply semantic-linguistics? Certainly Gadamer does not mean that only a formal grasp of the way a language works is required. The important thing is what is actually *said* in the language. Thus, because language is central to world-view, literature and the written word have an added importance for hermeneutic Verstehen (pp. 367 ff.). In the case of historico-cultural material which is less obviously language-related (not only purely visual objects, such as paintings, or dance, but also the scientific body of knowledge, political ideologies, etc. in which it does not seem to matter exactly how the idea is worded as much as what it says), the relevance of language is less direct but just as fundamental. If one is to understand a culture, in order to see the context of meaning of its particular aspects, the understanding of the language, as basic to and determining the world-view, is a primary requisite. And here, it is language in practice, rather than abstract grammar or lexicon, which is to be observed (p. 439). (Cf. Wittgenstein's view of language as a form of life, and Winch's development of Wittgenstein's philosophy, which more or less reduces social science to linguistic analysis (Winch 1971). Gadamer does not follow the argument to this extreme; we could say that he emphasises the centrality of language among other forms of life.) Because linguisticness characterises our human world-experience, it also characterises the exercise of the *wirkungsgeschichtliche Bewusstsein*. 'If we characterised above the method of execution of the effect-historical consciousness by its linguisticness, it was because linguisticness characterises overall our human world-experience' (p. 432). As Gadamer puts it, 'all our world experience, especially the hermeneutic experience, develops out of the centre of language'. And because of the linguisticness of hermeneutic interpretation, the latter is in a certain sense 'speculative' (p. 448), partly because what is actually said is always balanced in a dialectical relationship with what remains *un*said (cf. looking for the words to say what one means, for example), and partly because the interpreting word is the word of the interpreter, and not the language of the text—i.e. it is a *new* creation of Verstehen. Here, Gadamer abruptly turns back into ontology, in which he concludes the work. The speculative mode of being of language, he argues, demonstrates its universal ontological significance. ('Die spekulative Seinsart der Sprache erweist damit ihre universelle ontologische Bedeutung' (p. 450).)

The dialectical relationship of language and being therefore gives hermeneutics, based as it is on linguistic foundations, an ontological aspect, for just as language-understanding involves a certain 'grasp of being' (*Seinsverfassung*, p. 452) (with which what is actually said lies in a kind of tension), so this same grasp of being underlies hermeneutics. This is why Gadamer talks of 'language as the horizon of a hermeneutic ontology'. ('Sprache als Horizont einer hermeneutischen Ontologie' (chapter heading of Part III).) I find much of what Gadamer says in this final section difficult to comprehend and would reject a great deal of those parts which I do understand. Here, his belief in the Platonic ideals of absolute truth and beauty is more explicit; ideals to which we have access only by virtue of the 'light' (pp. 457–8) of the word, or of the beautiful, because of the finiteness of human existence. It is not particularly important, however, to suggest an alternative ontology, or to fault Gadamer's Platonism on specific points, despite the fact that he feels that ontology and method, truth and objectivity, are inseparable. His own conclusion is that, as Verstehen is *never* free of prejudices, and the being of the knower inevitably comes into play in his knowledge, it is clear that the scientific method, particularly in the cultural sciences, does not guarantee truth: 'There is certainly no Verstehen which is free from all prejudices. . . . Throughout our enquiry, it has been shown that the certainty which the use of scientific method provides is not enough to guarantee truth' (p. 465). Thus, having proved the limitations of method, we must rely on hermeneutics as the only possible mode of access to truth.

I want to follow this rather (although necessarily) lengthy exposition of Gadamer's ideas by several critical comments, both drawing from other writers who have taken Gadamer up on a number of points, and arising also from my own reading of his work. This should not be expected to be a complete and overall critique on all levels, however, but will be seen to have relevance to the central theoretical issues of this book, as outlined in earlier chapters. The intention is to extract from Gadamer's hermeneutic theory the elements of a sociology of knowledge without some of the deficiencies of existing theories in this tradition, and through a discussion of *Wahrheit und Methode* to re-define for our own purposes a hermeneutic sociology of art and literature.

To begin with the positive aspects of Gadamer's hermeneutics, which suggest the theory as an original and potentially adequate sociology of knowledge, some of the requirements which, in our earlier discussion, we have found crucial and which hermeneutic philosophy appears to fulfil are the following. First, it incorporates an explicit notion of 'cultural totality', of the unified and basic whole of a culture and a society at the level of the fundamental ideology or world-view, a notion which we saw to be problematic in the arguments of Gombrich, and unresolved in the theories of Mannheim, Lévi-Strauss, Goldmann and Parsons. Second, the place of art in social life is already defined, at least in a certain sense, in Gadamer's scheme, for, as I have shown, he begins his analysis of the relationship of the cultural sciences to the whole of life-experience with an examination of the specific relationship of art and aesthetic experience to human social existence. Thus the elaboration of a sociology of knowledge provides also a ready-made social theory of art. Third, many of the traditional problems of methodology in sociological theory, and particularly in the sociology of knowledge, are tackled by hermeneutic theory and, if we accept Gadamer's arguments in their entirety, definitive solutions presented. Foremost among these questions of method are: a new and detailed account of the nature of Verstehen as a methodological precept; the resolution of the problem of relativity, in a positive elaboration of the possibility of cross-cultural or trans-historical understanding (the 'over-stepping of horizons'); and a re-definition of 'objectivity' in the social sciences, in the light of the recognition by more recent sociologists that total elimination of the ego is impossible. Finally, there are at least suggestive implications of a theory of the constitution of consciousness itself, which, although primarily a question of the constitution of the existential reality of the individual, is nevertheless a related problem of the sociologist of knowledge. (Cf. Berger and Luckmann's analysis of the *social* construction of reality, Berger and Luckmann 1967.) Here too, the essential role of language in the creation of the world of meaning is considered and emphasised. For all these reasons Gadamer's theory must be taken seriously, for if it lives up to all its claims, it would go a long way towards providing a sociology of knowledge which, it is my argument, is needed at this stage.

It is worth stopping for a moment at this point, in order to recapitulate and summarise more exactly what an adequate sociology of art, as we have been attempting to define it, must be. Its object would be to make clear the social nature of art in terms of the expression *in* art of the total ideology, or world-view, or aspects of this world-view, of the social group in which it arises. This has been seen to involve the understanding of the social origin of ideology itself—in language, interaction and learned interpretations of the world. At the same time, it must be made clear *in what way* art can be said to express ideology, and the sociology of art must not, in considering extra-aesthetic aspects of creativity, abandon the central aesthetic perspective. That is, it must remain sensitive to the nature of art, and not, as has frequently been the case among sociologists, accept unquestioningly ready-made definitions and classifications of art, or fail to take into account the content of works of art. Finally, the whole analysis must be undertaken and phrased in language which is 'adequate at the level of meaning'. It is my contention that the hermeneutic perspective is a valuable contribution to such a theory, and I hope to suggest the elements of a hermeneutically based sociology of art in the next chapter. First, however, I shall propose five main criticisms of Gadamer's theory, again from the point of view of the central concerns of this book.

1   Gadamer is not a sociologist, and his philosophy, although it is intended to apply to the *Geisteswissenschaften* in general, is in fact applied by him exclusively to *historical* understanding. Our question

then is whether it *is* in fact equally applicable and useful in socio-logical understanding. The objection which immediately springs to mind is that the continuity of tradition, which unites the historian with his subject, and which is essential to the hermeneutic under-standing, is not such an obvious feature in contemporary sociological, particularly cross-cultural, analysis. Clearly, for the hermeneutic method to be appropriate in this area, the concept of the hermeneutic universal must be relevant here, for otherwise the interpreter must indeed either resort to the leap of intuitive self-transportation into another culture (since to bring his own with him in this case would surely be to *distort* the material with pre-definitions, and not to provide helpful, guiding prejudices for his research), or fall back on the more clinical and detached Verstehen through ideal types, or even non-verstehende analysis. Thus, we must begin by clarifying the scope of Gadamer's hermeneutic Verstehen.

The first point I want to make here is that the dividing line between history and sociology is not as clear-cut as academic defini-tions lead us to believe. There is, of course, something called history, which is in no way sociological (the history of wars, events, monar-chies, edicts, revolutions, etc. removed from their social background), just as some sociology is not at all historical (the sociology of a factory, the sociology of fashion or painting in the 1970s). But in which category are we to put, for example, the sociological study of eighteenth-century painting in England? It is apparent that there is an overlapping of discipline boundaries, and a fusion of interests and approaches, in the large and important area of historico-socio-cultural research. In this case, therefore, there is no problem in employing hermeneutic understanding in the study of eighteenth-century English art, for the continuity of tradition arises from the historical nature of the enquiry.

Two slightly different cases add their own complications to the possibility of a hermeneutic sociology. These are (a) the study of twentieth-century English painting; and (b) the study of eighteenth-century French painting. In neither example is it simply a case of historical interpretation within a tradition: (a) is not historical and (b) involves a *foreign* tradition. The first question is easily resolved, for the need for movement between periods or cultures does not arise; the interpreter is already inside the context of his material. His task, therefore, is merely to maintain the *wirkungsgeschichtliche Bewusstsein*—the historical consciousness—in order to see himself *and* his material in their place in time. With regard to the second case, we must examine more closely the notion of a tradition. In a certain sense, we (by which I mean English sociologists) *are* part of the same tradition as the eighteenth-century French artist; the European tradition, or more widely, the Western tradition, is common to both,

119

and, depending on how far back into history we wish to go, the separation into two distinct traditions is more or less relevant. On the other hand, one can point to certain obvious differences in tradition. Language, of course, is the most obvious. One might also oppose French rationalist, Cartesian philosophy to British empiricism over the last couple of centuries. The limits of a 'tradition' become less clear. Indeed, one can also discover a variety of traditions *within* a nation at a given time (based, for example, on class). But if it makes sense at all to talk about 'the tradition' of a society, it is clearly permissible to refer to the *common* tradition of England and France. The task of understanding eighteenth-century French society is not particularly problematic for the twentieth-century English sociologist, and the hermeneutic consciousness is able to extend to a culture which is foreign in some ways, but related to, and part of, the same broad tradition as that of the interpreter. The qualification here would be, presumably, that special care must be taken in the hermeneutic circle of anticipation-correction, for one will have to be particularly open to the otherness of the culture, and not allow the prejudices of enquiry to dictate the results.

This leaves only those cases of cross-cultural (historical or contemporary) investigation where the divergence of cultures is at a maximum. Our question here is whether it makes sense to advocate a hermeneutic anthropology. What point is there in advising the interpreter here to take into account his *own* historicity, or in emphasising the advantages his research will gain by his bringing into it prejudices originating in his own culture? One would be inclined to argue that such prejudices could only mislead the anthropologist, and could rarely be expected to aid his research. It was, in fact, one of the major mistakes made by the earliest anthropologists to approach an alien culture equipped with definitions, categories and expectations exported from their own society, and it was this type of practice which obviated a verstehende methodology in the study of primitive tribes. If the result of applying hermeneutics is merely to return to a less reputable anthropology, there would certainly be no justification for its use, and furthermore, Gadamer's claim that it is *the* method of all the cultural sciences would at least have to be modified. I would approach this problem in the following way. In the first place, there is *not* a straightforward dichotomous division between those cultures which are within the same common tradition as ourselves and those which are totally outside it. The distinction between Indo-European and other cultures is no basis for such a dichotomy and neither is any other categorisation in terms of historic/prehistoric origin. Just as other Western societies are all, in varied degrees, more or less part of the same tradition as our own, so can other cultures be seen as to a greater or lesser extent similar to our own. The more we have in common with another culture, the more will our own culturally conditioned prejudices guide us in our understanding of it. But here we must not forget Gadamer's insistence that hermeneutics is not simply a method or a tool for research, but that there are ontological justifications *for* the method. Hermeneutic understanding is both necessary and possible by virtue of the reality of being of interpreter and subjects, in particular their existence in a 'single horizon' (p. 288). If we accept the fact that there *is* a single horizon of all human life, then common humanity is in itself enough guarantee that the hermeneutic circle will work as well in the study of the primitive tribes of New Guinea as it does in European history, or the sociology of contemporary Britain. (However, unlike Gadamer, I would argue that whether or not, or to what extent, there *is* a common mode of thought, or existence, or of behaviour across cultures is a matter for investigation, and not ontological or metaphysical decision.) In conclusion, having agreed that the hermeneutic circle is useful *to the extent that* the two cultures coincide or run parallel, I would simply state that Gadamer is right. Inasmuch as prejudices *are* indeed the necessary conditions of experience, they cannot be abandoned, even in the case where one is sure that eventually they will have to be modified drastically. The concept of 'openness', of course, is crucial. The anticipated totality is tentatively projected on the material, and is immediately referred back for adjustment and modification. Through a prolonged process of projection-modification, a kind of objectivity is reached. The hermeneutic method, in short, is not restricted to historical investigation, but applies also in the cultural sciences where continuity of a single tradition is not a defining characteristic.

2 With regard to my second criticism, Gadamer cannot be so easily defended. Here I refer to a certain epistemological weakness of his whole theory, in particular his wholesale rejection of the Enlightenment, and of the principles of scientific theory. (Some of these arguments are put forward in a book by Apel, Habermas *et al.*, entitled *Hermeneutik und Ideologiekritik*, 1971.) Two of the points Gadamer makes *are* valid in this context: first, that the methods of the natural sciences are inadequate when it comes to understanding human and cultural phenomena, and second, that perception is socially and situationally conditioned, and that prejudices are thus inevitable accompaniments of all experience (including the interpretative study of culture). But as Emilio Betti points out, Gadamer, in rejecting at the same time all the other canons of science, leaves us with an unsatisfactory concept of 'objectivity' (Betti 1962). Betti's objection is that there is no reliable criterion for the *correctness* of our understanding (p. 41). He agrees that it is nonsensical to demand that the interpreter obliterates his own subjectivity, considering

121

subjective interpretation to be the most objective (p. 24). He feels that Gadamer takes the case too far, however, in advocating that the interpreter think *with* his own historicity. Betti argues that this leads to a loss of objectivity which is not counterbalanced by the interpreter's self-consciousness of his own historicity (p. 41). His account of an adequate hermeneutic understanding is that the present directs its interest, but stays out of the process. 'The present assists and encourages the noetic interest in Verstehen, but must stay out of action in the conversion of the subjective stance' (p. 46).

In other words, understanding a text does not involve mediation with the present. What Gadamer's theory guarantees is the *coherence* of the historical material, but not necessarily its *rightness* (p. 41). Betti goes on to suggest that what he calls a 'technical-morphological interpretation' (p. 57) meets the demands of the adequacy of meaning of Verstehen as well as satisfying the criterion of objectivity. This, briefly, consists in discovering the laws of development of the different forms of human culture (p. 56), going beyond a purely psychological interpretation, which in itself would fail to grasp the mode of operation (*Werkcharakter* (p. 58)) of institutions, styles, ways of thought. The historical or cultural object must be taken in its inner coherence in its context of meaning with related meaningful forms (p. 62). The premiss underlying Betti's recommendation of morphological interpretation is the lawfulness of intellectual forces (p. 60). Thus, the discovery of the laws of construction and development of the forms of human culture—its morphology—is supposed to add objectivity to interpretative Verstehen. The canons of objective understanding set out by Betti are thereby fulfilled—namely, the canon of the *hermeneutic autonomy* of the object (guaranteeing that it is understood in terms of its *own* alien spirit—*fremder Geist*); the canon of *meaningful coherence* (whereby the object is understood in its context); the canon of the *actuality of understanding* (by which the material is translated into the interpreter's own life actuality); and the canon of *meaning-equivalence* (between the process of creation of a work and the process of interpretation). The first three, followed by Gadamer, produce the right approach to cultural material, but only the fourth, ignored by him, guarantees objectivity.

We have endorsed Gadamer's statement that all perception and therefore all experience (including sociological interpretation) is relative. I take it that the sociologist must also subscribe to the need for 'objectivity' of one sort or another. Nevertheless, I believe that it goes beyond the confines of analytical and empirical reasoning to follow Gadamer from this point in locating objectivity in what I would argue is a speculative ontology. Therefore the objectivity of the hermeneutic interpretation must be guaranteed other than through an account of the nature of being of observer and subject. In this, Betti is surely correct. His solution is to suggest that to understand the historical context of our material we must understand its *Werkcharakter*, the structure in its *own* lawfulness, which objectively underlies it (p. 58). In other words, by paying more attention to structure, we will perceive the 'objective spirit' of the style of art, social institutions, or of the period itself. Betti's objections to the alternative 'psychological' interpretations can surely not be directed against Gadamer, for Gadamer is just as insistent as Betti on the contextual grasp of totalities (if not on their laws of development). Similarly, Betti's admonishment that the present, having played its essential part in directing interest, stays *out* of the process of interpretation is rather beside the point, particularly in the light of his own reference to the interpreter's adaptation in his own experience of his material (the third canon). I cannot see, in fact, that a better concept of objectivity is to be found in Betti's version of hermeneutics; the mere invocation of that divinity, Structure, and its related concept of morphology, does not seem to me to provide the answer.

Having said that, however, I am unable myself to present a new solution. It seems to me that the abandonment of the old and respected scientific notion of objectivity, and of the philosophical idea of the thing-in-itself, leaves us only with the possibility of falling back on Weber's injunction of empirical verification, which, one might argue, is more or less what Gadamer, in his different language, means by recommending 'openness' to the facts. We cannot, it appears, go any further than a rigorous examination and recognition of our own prejudices, and the testing and re-testing of our interpretations by reference to the data. Here I would quote Paul Bohannan, from another context (that of the anthropology of legal systems) whose statement of the epistemological problem I fully endorse (1969, p. 407).

> There is, of course, no possibility of ever arriving at a 'fact' that is uncolored by the ethnographic instrument, the perceiver of the fact. The concrete system necessarily remains a mystery. All we can do is to learn more about our sensory means of perception, and mechanical and other extrinsic extensions of them, and our own cultural prison. Communication to a degree is possible, and it is the wish of most parties in most situations to refine that degree.

3 I said earlier that it was one of the merits of Gadamer's analysis that it incorporates a theory of the constitution of consciousness, a theory, as I have tried to show, which is essential to the sociology of knowledge. Here I must add that his theory does not go

far enough, and that certain crucial aspects of the fundamental co-ordinates of experience are omitted altogether. In fairness, of course, it should be said that it is not Gadamer's primary objective to present a systematic theory of knowledge and perception. His insight is to recognise, in the course of his investigation of related problems of knowledge and experience, certain essential elements of consciousness. In particular, he confirms the perspectivism of all perception; he argues for the contribution of language in the creation of the world; and he emphasises the inevitable historical and social determinants of experience. My chief objection is to the *idealism* of this view (and thus, as a corollary, of his general theory of hermeneutics). In incorporating many of the important insights of Hegel into his own theory, he reverts at the same time to that Hegelian view of history which Marx and Weber so convincingly and (one would have thought) definitively attacked. One gets the impression, from *Wahrheit und Methode*, of an independently existing language (or languages) by courtesy of which the human being is permitted limited access to the real world. Without denying the linguistic relativity of experience, I am arguing that to stop at this point explains nothing about the true constitution of consciousness, for language is *not* an independently existing, unalterable and primary entity. We must go beyond language, and other 'ideal' factors, to the *material* basis of existence, and to the social relations underlying it (see chapter 2(iii)).

Habermas (1970) offers his own particular version of Marxist theory as a corrective to Gadamer's idealism. He too argues that linguistic-hermeneutic sociology is inadequate, as it provides no way for the sociologist to go *beyond* cultural symbols. For example, one might want to explain *changes* in speech patterns (p. 293). To do so, he proposes the necessity for a return to a type of *functionalist* analysis (p. 305). In particular, the fundamental factors of *work* and *authority* are to be added to language as the basic objective context of human life (p. 289). The advantage of a functionalist approach, as he sees it, is that *non*-normative elements can also be given their due. The dimensions of work and authority are not to be suppressed in favour of subjective symbolic content (p. 305). The result is a hermeneutically enlightened and historically directed functionalism (p. 306), which does not make the mistake of assuming that linguistic consciousness determines material existence.

Habermas's ideas about the determining power of work, language and authority are more fully elaborated elsewhere (e.g. Habermas 1966 and 1972). As he claims these to be the three fundamental factors defining experience, it would be well worth examining the analysis, to determine whether it does indeed provide an adequate account of social life. However, that cannot be attempted here, the main point being that Habermas has seen the philosophical prejudice which underlies and distorts Gadamer's theory of knowledge and experience. I would argue, too, that the origin of consciousness must finally be traced back to the material factors in social life, and to the social interaction processes which arise therefrom. In this context, Berger and Luckmann's account of the social construction of reality suggests one way in which the idealism of Gadamer's hermeneutics can be corrected.

4 An integral part of Gadamer's philosophy is his Hegelian concept of the cultural totality of an age and of a society, and this, I have argued, has been a stumbling block for many other writers in the sociology of knowledge and the philosophy of art, being on the one hand, extremely difficult to define or locate, and on the other, crucial to a theory of cultural history or sociology. Nevertheless, Gadamer's attempt to resolve the dilemma is not quite what is needed, although it is certainly on the right lines, and is a great improvement on the self-imposed limitations of thought and imagination of non-Hegelian thinkers. To begin with, there is a certain ambiguity in the concept of 'whole' or 'totality'. Its various meanings appear to include: the whole of meaning; the whole of life, represented in a moment; the projected meaning of the whole of a text or a language in the context of which its constituent parts may be understood and interpreted; and the whole of history, uniting observer with observed. The nature of the fundamental 'totality' is not clarified further by the workings of the hermeneutic circle (with its own ambiguity, referred to above), for the totality which is projected in the circular process is sometimes seen to be a text, sometimes a general historical setting and sometimes a context even more vaguely specified. Despite the looseness of terminology and indeterminateness of reference, I feel that Gadamer's idea of cultural 'wholes' is worth rescuing. If this concept itself is too amorphous to be useful in his work, the related concept of a 'horizon' is more promising. Here we have a more stable notion of the existential-historical situation, whether of an actor, a work of art or a text, or a social institution. It makes sense, then, to talk about the movement from one horizon (interpreter's present) to another (the past of his research) and to introduce the idea of the *fusion* of two horizons. And here lies the importance of insisting on *meaning* as the frame of reference, as I have done throughout this essay. It is only by retaining the existential-phenomenological perspective that cultural history/sociology is in a position to discover such horizons which, whatever their origins in economic or other material factors may be, express essentially the life-world of the members of that culture. (One could put this another way by showing the absurdity of relating, say, a literary work, prose or poetry, directly to the class structure of society,

without referring to the crucial mediating factor of *consciousness* of class, which alone would render class potent as an operative agent in creativity.)

What is most striking about the hermeneutic approach to cultural history is that the problem of the cultural totality is simply and effectively solved by making it a *premiss* of the theory. The Hegelian view of history has a built-in notion of supra-individual units, and Gadamer, by adopting this perspective and blending it with post-Husserlian phenomenology, does not ask whether there *are* cultural unities, but proceeds on the assumption that indeed there are. In Hegel's philosophy, and particularly in the work of some of his disciples, as Gombrich has shown (see chapter 4 above), the premiss was eventually abused, and turned to illegitimate metaphysical proofs. The question arises, therefore, whether this is inevitable, and whether Gadamer's historical method itself relies on metaphysics. Is he, too, guilty of performing the unjustified leap from the *personal* existential horizon to that of a social *group*?

My conclusion on this controversial problem is that this is in fact the *only* way cultural history can proceed. Although it remains true that a social world-view cannot be shown to exist (in its unity, coherence and consistency) in the same way as Husserl and Merleau-Ponty have demonstrated the nature of the Lebenswelt of the indivi-dual, and although there is no reason to assume a *single* world-view for a complex group, it is methodologically both permissible and necessary to posit such a world-view. Here, Gadamer's hermeneutic circle, with the guidance of the *wirkungsgeschichtliche Bewusstsein*, serves to help the historian/sociologist, and to adjust the postulated world-view until it comes as closely as possible in line with reality. Metaphysics is perfectly respectable, in the service of poetry, and (what is more or less the same thing, in terms of imagination and suggestion, if not of purpose) in the role of creating new models of perception—for perception, it has been argued, is never naïvely pure. It transcends the boundaries of this role when it mistakes models of comprehension for ontological statements about the world, or extracts from them ethical and political imperatives. To the extent that Gadamer extends methodology and epistemology into ontology, he is guilty of this. I have shown, however, that this failing can be separated from the main body of his theory, which stands as a valuable contribution to the sociology of culture. On the question of cultural 'wholes', his account is deficient only in clarity (lack of ambiguity) and detail (an adequate description of the 'cultural horizon' of an age): the basic conception is admirable, and— Gadamer's major originality in this field—his exposition of the hermeneutic method in dealing with world-views, together with their relation to particular facts and expressions, is an important and enlightening theoretical achievement, unattainable by the approaches considered above.

5 The final point I want to make with regard to Gadamer's contribution to the sociology of art and literature concerns the place of art in the wider category of 'knowledge' and in its relation to social life. This is something I shall deal with in the following chapter, and here I shall only briefly mention what I consider to be the deficiencies of Gadamer's theory.

Although he devotes a disproportionately large section of his book to aesthetic theory, he does not provide an adequate account either of the relationship between artistic expression and life and the life-world, or of the nature of expression in forms of art. The purpose of his detailed analysis of art and of the aesthetic experience is primarily to illustrate in its most obvious form the argument for a unique mode of knowledge for the *Geisteswissenschaften*, by revealing the limitations of the natural-scientific approach in cultural areas. From the analysis of the experience of art, he sets out to develop 'a concept of knowledge and truth which corresponds to the whole of our hermeneutic experience'. But the second and third sections, where this general hermeneutic experience is developed, hardly ever refer back to art, and there is no explicit definition of the place of aesthetic experience and creativity in the hermeneutic universe. There is only a short discussion, in the first section, on the nature of experience (*Erlebnis*) as such (pp. 63 ff.), where Gadamer argues that any experience is united, by its intentional content, in an 'unmediated relationship with the totality of life', that it is, in his words, the 'representation of the whole in a moment'. (By life, he means the particular life of the individual, and not a more abstract concept, or supra-individual totality.) Aesthetic experience, he goes on, is no different in this respect; it, too, represents the *total* meaning of life. The world of art, then, is to be understood as the completion of the symbolic representation of life, to which each experience leads. Then follows the thesis which I have outlined above; namely that aesthetic abstraction overlooks the essentially historical nature of the aesthetic experience, and its continuity and unity with the life of the historical spirit, and that in returning art to its true place in the world of events, we are enabled to understand ourselves in the world of the work of art (p. 92). He concludes that art is knowledge, and the experience of a work of art is sharing in this knowledge (ibid.).

My objection is not that Gadamer is wrong to recommend the transcending of the aesthetic dimension; as I hope I have already made clear, I strongly endorse this precept as leading to a fuller comprehension of the nature of artistic expression. Rather, I feel that he does not develop his own aesthetics satisfactorily, but leaves the reader with only a number of unsystematised hints as to the essence of art, and its relation to life-experience. Even in the following section concerning the ontology of the work of art, where we might expect clarification on this question, his sole theme is the essential contemporaneity of art—the fact that its representation, or reception by an audience, is as much a part of its being as its original creation. We are never told what it is of historical existence which is expressed in art, nor the mode of this expression. (There is a brief reference to signs and symbols (pp. 137 ff.) where Gadamer states that a painting is something *between* the two, neither purely referring away to something else, nor purely standing in for something else. But this can hardly be considered an adequate theory of symbolic reference.) The hermeneutic theory of ideology (that is, of all knowledge) must be supplemented with an aesthetics which does not merely, as Gadamer's does, take art to be one of the many interconnected features of cultural life, but which makes explicit this connection.

These then, are my chief criticisms of *Wahrheit und Methode*, in the context of the specific interests of this study. I would repeat here the disclaimer I have already made once, that my purpose is not to subject to critical analysis Gadamer's notion of 'truth' and its attendant ontological theory. This, although crucial to his own philosophy, is neither a necessary foundation for those of his arguments we have been considering, nor relevant to the terms of reference of this study. In the final chapter, I shall review the arguments of the book and, summarising the contributions of hermeneutic philosophy and its relevance to the preceding chapters, suggest the theoretical framework for a hermeneutic sociology of knowledge and art.

8 Conclusion: towards a hermeneutic sociology of art

The sociology of art and literature, as a branch of the sociology of knowledge, shares the theoretical orientation of the latter as well as its problems of method and philosophy. In addition it faces other difficulties, theoretical, conceptual and procedural, which are specific to the subject. I am suggesting here that hermeneutics as a method and a philosophy has much to contribute to the resolution of many of these issues. Incorporating the advantages of both the structural approach and, particularly, the phenomenological perspective, hermeneutic sociology is in a position to comprehend the diversity of levels of analysis as well as the various, and often contradictory, aspects of knowledge, in a dialectical, sophisticated framework which does not need to abandon the level of meaning as the essential element of sociological understanding. The deficiencies of the hermeneutic method itself, referred to in the preceding chapter, are not necessarily inherent *in* the approach, and may, to a large extent, be removed by critique and revision. This concluding chapter will attempt to outline such a hermeneutic sociology of knowledge in the context of the arguments of the earlier chapters of the book.

In chapters 3 and 4 the questions discussed were, on the whole, questions of the philosophy and method of sociology; dialectical hermeneutics, itself a method for the cultural sciences, supplies answers to these questions. But hermeneutics is more than a methodology. As a philosophical theory of knowledge, it is also equipped to incorporate the analyses of chapter 2—that is, of the constitution of knowledge itself, both of the sociologist and of the social individual. Furthermore, and this is perhaps its unique and primary importance, the very fact that it combines epistemology with theory and methodology in this way gives it an enormous advantage over traditional theories, which, as I argued earlier (chapter 3), are handicapped by conventional boundaries of discipline. I have already

129

listed briefly (pp. 117–18 above) the merits of a hermeneutic approach to the sociology of knowledge, and have also suggested some of the ways in which hermeneutics, as expounded by Gadamer, may be supplemented in order to correct its own failings. My argument throughout has been that only the phenomenological perspective is equipped to provide a philosophically sound basis for the sociology of knowledge, but that there are certain disadvantages and limitations inherent in a pure phenomenology of the social world. Phenomenological hermeneutics combines the positive features of this approach with a complementary sociological (structural) and historical (diachronic) model, thus avoiding the most damaging criticisms of phenomenological sociology.

The sociology of knowledge explores the social co-ordinates of all forms of knowledge. This very brief, however, presupposes the relativity, in some sense and to some extent, *of* knowledge: that is, the fact that knowledge is not absolute, and is itself constituted in the mind. I have argued that it is the phenomenological analysis of consciousness which demonstrates the existential quality of knowledge and of all mental phenomena (chapter 2(i)), as well as the inner coherence of the Lebenswelt of the individual. The important constituting effect of language on thought and knowledge is a crucial element in the examination of the foundations of consciousness (chapter 2(ii)) and this, as we have seen, is not overlooked either by the hermeneutics of Gadamer or by the hermeneutic sociology of Habermas. Third, the more obvious social co-ordinates of knowledge (the usual categories of the sociology of knowledge) must be incorporated (chapter 2(iii)). Habermas's sociology (Habermas 1970), which moves from positivism through phenomenology, linguistic analysis and hermeneutics, to a revised materialism-functionalism relating knowledge to language, work and authority, is an example of an account which successfully includes the various determining influences on thought.

The next series of questions which the sociology of knowledge must consider are reflexive ones; in other words, they concern the sociologist's own methodology and the possibility of his actually being able to practise a sociology of knowledge. These problems of method and of epistemology were reviewed in chapter 3. In considering them, it is necessary to turn from pure phenomenology to other theoretical frameworks, although phenomenology does have its own original contribution to make here too. (See, for example, Schutz's account of sociological understanding, Schutz 1972.) The historicism of Dilthey is one way of overcoming (or perhaps merely ignoring) the problem of relativity and of dealing with historical understanding. The philosophy of (for example) Scheler answers philosophical questions of relativity and reality. Mannheim, Parsons and Gurvitch all suggest different schemata for differentiating the types of knowledge (less a philosophical or epistemological problem than a conceptual and methodological one). Kantian and neo-Kantian ontology defines the limits of knowledge of reality, and in so doing defines 'reality'. Each of these theories is open to criticism in its own area. But, in any case, the object is to develop a sociology which can deal with all these questions itself. Again, my contention is that a hermeneutic sociology can best do this. The relativity of the sociology of knowledge is no longer seen as a vicious circle, but becomes the very condition of understanding. Objectivity finally abandons its hopeless claim to absoluteness, and is re-defined as historically and socially bound. The ontological question of reality is less successfully handled by Gadamer, particularly in his more unequivocally idealist moments, but the fundamental hermeneutic conception, not followed to this extreme, implies a non-paradoxical definition of 'reality' in its premiss of the *Daseins*-relativity of the world, and the historical nature of truth. The tension between structure and the existential individual is also resolved, for hermeneutics retains the phenomenological perspective in considering cultural totalities (p. 103 above). The concepts of the hermeneutic circle and the *wirkungsgeschichtliche Bewusstsein* together serve to eliminate all those problems which a non-dialectical, absolutist or single-level analysis can only see as paradoxes.

The next three chapters (chapters 4–6) considered the problematic concept of a world-view, and examined some attempts to define this. Here the phenomenology of consciousness does indeed prove inadequate in the comprehension of a supra-individual consciousness. Structural approaches, on the other hand, suffer from the disadvantage that, abandoning the level of meaning which phenomenology inhabits, they have no way of identifying either the pertinent groups to which an ideology or world-view may be attributed, or the nature and relevant content of such world-views. The identification of these groups becomes a matter of arbitrary decision or prior commitment. (See my discussion of Goldmann, chapter 5(ii) above.) Other sociological theories of ideology whose references to Weltanschauungen and their elements rest on formal abstractions or psychologistic generalisations are equally suspect in their grasp of the meaning-component of social world-views. I have argued that the dialectical approach of hermeneutic sociology allows it to grasp structural wholes while referring simultaneously to existential meanings of historical individuals. It is because the frame of reference of meaning is retained that the premiss of cultural unity becomes permissible. In part, the assumption is a metaphor, and a working hypothesis which is tested in the empirical examination of the facts. But, more than this, it is a unity *by definition*, for Gadamer *asserts* that we are dealing with cultural totalities and that the major problem

131

is *how* we do this. This is legitimate in the hermeneutic context as it was not in the cultural history criticised by Gombrich or in the structural-functionalism of Talcott Parsons (chapter 6(iv)), for here the unity and coherence are guaranteed by the phenomenological foundation of *meaning*. Neither is this achieved by a theoretical jump from individual Lebenswelt to group ideology, for Gadamer *begins* with the culture and not the individual, and only then performs the phenomenological analysis of its elements and constituents. (This may be seen as an elaboration of the suggestions made by Mannheim (chapter 4(i)), who nevertheless was not able to resolve the circularity of the method himself.) His version of phenomenology, of course, is rather remote from the pure phenomenology of consciousness of Husserl, working as it does within the essentially historicist framework of cultural history. Similarly, it goes beyond the micro-level of analysis of Schutz, Berger and more recent phenomenological sociologists in a reversion to a Hegelian perspective of society and the individual. Nevertheless, his initial claim to combine Dilthey's historicism and Heidegger's existentialism with Husserl's phenomenology withstands attack. Hermeneutics consists in the end in the individual, socially-situated, sociologist or historian understanding the existential meanings, symbols, expressions and values of another culture and its inhabitants, and simultaneously aware of his own historical consciousness and its role in this process.

The hermeneutic approach to cultural history and Weltanschauungs-theory avoids the pitfalls which in the end undermine the otherwise admirable and highly suggestive theories of both Mannheim and Goldmann, and in so doing fulfils the implicit promise of the possibility of a sociology of world-views. All three theories start with the same basic insight, namely that the social and cultural totality is something *sui generis*, over and above the world-view of individuals and more than simply, for example, the religious belief-system of a society. All three also agree in refusing to grant any mystical or metaphysical reality to the social ideology or Weltanschauung, and in insisting on its ultimate dependence on, or origin in, the actions and interactions of individuals. In each case, the dialectical relationship of the parts and the whole is recognised, and, as a corollary to this, the necessity of a dialectical and dynamic mode of comprehension of world-views, their elements and expressions, and the particular members of the relevant society. I have argued that both Mannheim and Goldmann ultimately fail in this attempt. In Mannheim's case, there is no solution to the methodological problem of the circularity of procedures of understanding the elements of a culture in its total context and of grasping the totality *via* its elements. The dialectical vision here is only incipient, and neither sophisticated enough nor well enough understood to deal with the apparent contradictions of investigation. Goldmann is also, although to a lesser extent, open to this criticism. In another sense, his own scheme suffers from oversimplification too; the need to delimit important groupings (namely classes) in advance indicates that the model is not sensitive enough to the multitude of relevant substrata of world-views and artistic creativity. Similarly, the restriction of world visions to unified and cohesive groups is an unnecessary limitation for a comprehensive sociology of literature and of ideology. Gadamer's hermeneutic philosophy of history broadens the perspective of the interpreter, and completes the phenomenological theory of ideology. The crucial insight of hermeneutics which rescues Weltanschauungs-theory from both metaphysical conjecture and arbitrary legislation is the *tentative* nature of the projected totality, which is hypothetically (although based on more or less evidence or experience) projected, and then adjusted, amended, corrected and qualified in the light of the particular observations made and the specific manifestations subsequently apprehended. It hardly matters that the initial postulation of a total ideology or world-view is in no way 'scientific' or that its perception is journalistic or impressionistic in style. On the contrary, this is the very nature of understanding 'from the inside' of a culture, and is the essence, if not in rigour and reliability, of the phenomenological or verstehende grasp of the cultural world. The hermeneutic method of continual checking and re-checking both serves as the guarantee of correctness and eliminates the paradox of precedence of whole or parts.

These, then, are some of the chief problems of the sociology of knowledge, its theory and methodology. The concept of a world-view is particularly relevant to the sociology of art and literature, for the claim is often made that art expresses world-view. Thus a sociological theory which can incorporate this concept is already in an advantageous position as far as the sociology of art is concerned. One which does so, as does hermeneutics, within a phenomenological, verstehende orientation also fulfils the requirements I have suggested are essential for the proper sociological understanding of the arts (chapter 1). By referring constantly to the meanings of the artist, his work and his society, the sociology of art cannot fail to take account of the nature of art itself, and the aesthetics of the work of art; the relationship of these artistic meanings to the world of the artist and his audience will also be an intrinsic part of the analysis. Neverthe-less, as I have indicated, Gadamer does not develop his own theory of art and society, or describe exactly the place of aesthetic experience in the hermeneutic universe. He states that any experience is united with the totality of life, and it is this insight of phenomenological hermeneutics which, applied to art, would be the foundation of the type of sociology of art proposed in this book. The relationship of art

133

to the total existential reality, accounted for by Schutz on the individual level in his theory of the 'multiple realities' of the Lebenswelt, may thus be perceived sociologically, in the context of supra- (or trans-) individual subjects. Such a theory is contained in Gadamer's work, but it remains to be worked out more explicitly.

In conclusion, some tentative suggestions may be made as to how a hermeneutic sociology of knowledge, and a hermeneutic sociology of art, would proceed. Clearly it is beyond the scope of this work to present a fully worked out theory and method, and the preceding chapters cannot claim to have done more than prepare the foundations of such an approach. Neither is it possible to undertake here a full-scale study in the sociology of art or of literature on the lines of the approach advocated. My comments in this summary must remain sketchy, and my examples unelaborated. Nevertheless, it is probably most useful to outline the elements of a hermeneutic sociology of art by means of an example, however imperfectly the study may be executed. The example I have chosen here is the modern dance in contemporary Western society. Inasmuch as the major part of such a study would be the comprehension of the society of origin and existence of the modern dance form, and the forms of 'knowledge' of that society, then our investigation is an exercise in the sociology of knowledge. The rest of the analysis—namely the aesthetic, art-historical, and symbolic–expressive aspects of the dance itself—moves the level of investigation on to the more specific ground of the sociology of the arts. I have divided the analysis, somewhat arbitrarily, into four basic sections: (1) the hermeneutic grasp of the society of genesis of the modern dance; (2) the nature of modern dance itself; (3) the perspective of choreographer, dancer, and, perhaps, audience; and (4) the hermeneutic-phenomenological comprehension of the dynamics of changing dance-forms. I should point out that I am here concerned specifically with modern ballet—the dance tradition which both continues and revolutionises the tradition of the classical ballet, incorporating influences from outside the ballet (for example, from primitive dance, as in the work of Martha Graham), and now apparently co-existing, with more or less interaction, with the classical tradition. (This is exemplified in the repertoire of the Ballet Rambert in London and Bejart's Ballet of the Twentieth Century in Belgium, as well as in the inclusion recently of such modern works as Glen Tetley's *Field figures* in the programme of the Royal Ballet at Covent Garden.) I am referring to the various branches of a contemporary performing activity, which, like the opera and classical ballet, is confined to theatre presentation, restricted to a certain social élite, or at least minority, and involves rigorous training and certain competitive standards of ability, and not, for example, to untrained (though often equally stylised) non-performative, social dancing at parties, television pop programmes, and rock concerts. (There is, of course, no reason why a study of the role and nature of this form of dance could not also be undertaken sociologically; indeed, in some respects it would have certain advantages over the narrower 'high art' form I am discussing, in that its relevance to society and social life in general might be expected to be more obvious, more widespread, and thus more accessible, in not being limited to a small sector of the community.)

1   This part of the enquiry is the direct outcome of the arguments of this book; its results are the sociological understanding of knowledge and of the world-view of the society in question. It is also the most difficult to undertake. To begin with, one is confronted with the problem of where to delimit the society itself; this might be a national, economic, religious, continental, hemi-spherical (e.g. modern dance in its occidental context) or any other definition. The guiding advice of the hermeneutic method is *not* to define any such social grouping in advance (as one could argue Goldmann tends to do), but to understand the period and to be or become an insider in interpreting the life-world of its members (with the added bonus of the sociologist/ historian's clairvoyance of a supra-individual perspective and the ability to over-view society to a greater extent than can its average member). Only from this point of view can one obtain the crucial insights into the *significant* (in Goldmann's sense of the word) factors of social life and their expression in language, action and creativity, insights which are not to be obtained from a pre-conceived philosophy of history (materialist, idealist, or any other) which legislates blindly on the complex question of significant groups. A most important advantage of the hermeneutic-phenomenological approach, too, is its ability to perceive the relevance of group overlaps and group conflicts; it is not confined to one level of association or to coincidental boundaries, but can refer at once to the national and religious affiliations of individuals, whether or not these are co-extensive. In this manner, the cultural totality is projected, and the way left open for the relative weights and importance of its many features to be recognised, whether these be class, language, religion, arts, kinship systems. The projected totality, perhaps not even formulated and unconsciously understood, remains susceptible to correction and modification in the face of new evidence adduced or observations made. Thus, in the case of modern ballet, the society under discussion is indeed the modern Western world, with the emphasis perhaps on the United States from the 1920s, but certainly with reference to European countries where modern dance grew up independently and where it was accepted and acclaimed on crossing the Atlantic. (The cross-cultural sociological study of knowledge and ideology might be able to demonstrate why Great Britain lagged

forty years behind the United States in this, for the Graham Company's first visit to this country in the 1950s made very little impression, whereas her re-appearance more than ten years later was a great success.) This initial analysis, then, attempts to suggest the important characteristics (including historical factors of technological, material, urban, etc., change) of social life in America and Great Britain. It is open to the objection that it is impressionistic and unscientific, but can retort that the test is in the explanatory scope and potential of its final results. In the meantime, it is in a position to note *any* aspect of society which has a determining influence on thought and creativity.

2   The next section of the enquiry deals with the intrinsic features of the dance. This would be primarily descriptive. The fundamentals of the technique must be outlined, perhaps in contrast to the classical tradition from which it broke away. (For example, the opposition of weight, fall and gravity to elevation and lightness, or of contraction and release of back and hips to the rigid straightness of classical ballet would be discussed.) The mode of expression of the medium would have to be explored: its method of representation and story-telling, its incorporation of allegory, drama and emotion. It is also important to refer to the relationship of contemporary dance to the other contemporary arts, and to mixed media presentations. For example, the American choreographers Paul Taylor and Merce Cunningham have often collaborated with composer John Cage and artist-designer Robert Rauschenberg in the creation of their works. Similarly, many so-called modern ballets involve the use of film, slides, voice and other non-dance elements. Finally, the place of the dance in society and social life must be considered, including its place and method of presentation, the composition of its audiences, the choice and training of its performers, the role of the critic and its relation to other relevant facts of social life.

3   In this section the actual creation of dance is directly understood on the micro-level of phenomenological analysis. The place of dance in the Lebenswelt can thus be seen, for in the case of the individual choreographer, dancer and audience-member, the meaning of the dance in the context of his total life-world presents no problems of sociological generalisations, assumptions or theoretical constructions.

4   Finally, the sociologist is in a position to offer a hermeneutic-phenomenological account of the dance in contemporary society. By virtue of the uniqueness of the hermeneutic method, followed in the first part of the investigation, the final results should be able to record all those features of social life, apart from the intrinsic historical facts of the development of the art form, which do in fact have some influence on or reflection in the dance.

It is, I think, worth mentioning that the method I have been putting

136

forward, despite its obvious difficulties arising from the complexity of modern societies, is more or less that practised by anthropologists of art. In the case of primitive societies, the procedure is often exactly as outlined above. The anthropologist immerses himself in the culture, learns the language, the rules of behaviour, the practices and institutions. Only from this understanding, from this inside position, can he then begin to describe the art of that society and its expressive, symbolic, ritual and even unconscious significance (see, for example, Strathern and Strathern 1971, and Faris 1972).

The value of the hermeneutic perspective in the sociology of knowledge, and its advantages over other theories discussed in these chapters, should be apparent. It is able to work on any level, from the individual to the small group or the whole society. In the case of the individual, it is equivalent to a phenomenology of existence, but, like Schutz, and unlike the pure phenomenologists of consciousness, it perceives the social co-ordinates of the Lebenswelt. In addition, its historical perspective permits it to comprehend this life-world *dynamically* and *genetically*; that is, consciousness is not simply taken as given and as static, but is understood in its creation. The role of language, social relations, interests and (in a revised version of Gadamer's hermeneutics) material factors in the constitution of knowledge is clarified in the dynamic and dialectical version of phenomenological sociology. (One might say that the genetic phenomenology of consciousness becomes the sociology of knowledge; phenomenology itself is not concerned with the derivation of the data of the mind.) In the case of the social group, of whatever size, the sociologist or cultural historian begins with a projected image of the group in its totality of meanings which, at the outset, is not, and does not need to be, justified, but which is tested and adjusted in the subsequent investigations. This is simply to say that in approaching a culture we *do* have some prior indication (or prejudice) which guides our research; Goldmann's original decision to consider the relative importance of social classes as significant groupings is one example. With this initial orientation, the various elements and sub-sectors of the culture can be approached and understood, both in their cultural and in their historical contexts. (In this, the historicity of the researcher himself has certain implications for his method of investigation, as well as for the epistemological nature of his results.) On this macro-level, particularly, the sociology of art and literature can thrive. Works of art, styles, groups of artists, indeed everything relevant to the aesthetic sphere of human existence, are accessible to the sociological understanding in which the phenomenological comprehension of meanings is combined with the structural-historical comprehension of cultural totalities. The latter makes possible a conception of a transindividual subject and a transindividual world-view; the former demonstrates the inter-relations of art and the rest of culture. The dialectical hermeneutics of art and society enables the sociologist to explore both the origin of knowledge in social life, and the expression of such knowledge in the aesthetic sphere.

Bibliography

ALBRECHT, M. (1954) 'The relationship of literature and society', *American Journal of Sociology*, 59, 5.
ALBRECHT, M. (1956) 'Does literature reflect common values?', *American Sociological Review*, 21, 6.
ALTICK, R. D. (1957) *The English common reader: a social history of the mass reading public 1800–1900*, University of Chicago Press.
ANTAL, FREDERICK (1947) *Florentine painting and its social background*, Kegan Paul, London.
APEL, K.-O. (1971) 'Szientistik, Hermeneutik, Ideologiekritik. Entwurf einer Wissenschaftslehre in erkenntnisanthropologischer Sicht', in APEL *et al.*, *Hermeneutik und Ideologiekritik (q.v.)*.
APEL, K.-O. *et al.* (1971) *Hermeneutik und Ideologiekritik*, Suhrkamp Verlag, Frankfurt am Main.
BECKER, OSKAR (1962) 'Die Fragwürdigkeit der Transzendierung der ästhetischen Dimension der Kunst', *Philosophische Rundschau*, 10.
BENDA, C. E. (1959) 'The linguistic basis of consciousness', *E.T.C. A review of general semantics*, 16.
BENSMAN, J. and LILIENFELD, R. (1968) 'A phenomenological model of the artistic and critical attitudes', *Philosophy and Phenomenological Research*, 28.
BERGER, JOHN (1969) *Art and revolution: Ernst Neizvestny and the role of the artist in the USSR*, Weidenfeld & Nicolson, London.
BERGER, PETER (1967) *The sacred canopy: elements of a sociological theory of religion*, Doubleday, Garden City, N.Y.
BERGER, PETER L. and LUCKMANN, T. (1967) *The social construction of reality*, Allen Lane, London.
BERKELEY, GEORGE (1962) *The principles of human knowledge* (1710) *and Three dialogues between Hylas and Philonous* (1713), Wm Collins, London.
BERNSTEIN, B. (1971) *Class, codes and control.* Vol. 1: *Theoretical studies towards a sociology of language*, Routledge & Kegan Paul, London.
BERTALANFFY, L. VON (1955) 'Essay on the relativity of categories', *Philosophy of Science*, 22.

139

BIBLIOGRAPHY

BETTI, EMILIO (1962) *Die Hermeneutik als allgemeine Methodik der Geisteswissenschaften*, J. C. B. Mohr (Paul Siebeck), Tübingen.

BLUM, ALAN F. (1971) 'The corpus of knowledge as a normative order', in YOUNG, MICHAEL F. D. (ed.), *Knowledge and control. New directions for the sociology of education*, Collier-Macmillan, London.

BOHANNAN, PAUL (1969) 'Ethnography and comparison in legal anthropology', in NADER, LAURA (ed.), *Law in culture and society*, Aldine Publishing Company, Chicago.

BOTTOMORE, T. (1956) 'Some reflections on the sociology of knowledge', *British Journal of Sociology*, VII.

BROWN, D. W. (1960) 'Does language structure influence thought?', *E.T.C. A review of general semantics*, 17.

BROWN, R. (1958) *Words and Things*, Free Press, Chicago.

BROWN, R. and LENNEBERG, E. H. (1954) 'A study in language and cognition', *Journal of Abnormal and Social Psychology*, 49.

BROWN, R. and LENNEBERG, E. H. (1958) 'Studies in linguistic relativity', in MACCOBY, E., NEWCOMB, T. M. and HARTLEY, E. L. (eds), *Readings in social psychology*, Holt, New York.

CARMICHAEL, L., HOGAN, H. P. and WALTER, A. A. (1932) 'An experimental study of the effect of language on the reproduction of visually perceived form', *Journal of Experimental Psychology*, XV.

CARROLL, J. (1964) *Language and thought*, Prentice-Hall Inc., Englewood Cliffs, N.J.

CARROLL, J. B. and CASAGRANDE, J. B. (1958) 'The function of language classifications in behavior', in MACCOBY, E., NEWCOMB, T. M. and HARTLEY, E. L. (eds), *Readings in social psychology*, Holt, New York.

CASSIRER, E. (1933) 'Le langage et la construction du monde des objets', *Journal de Psychologie Normale et Pathologique*, 30.

CASSIRER, E. (1953) *Language and myth*, Dover, New York.

CAWS, PETER (1970) 'What is structuralism?', in HAYES and HAYES (eds), *Claude Lévi-Strauss: the anthropologist as hero (q.v.)*.

CHOMSKY, N. (1968) *Language and mind*, Harcourt, Brace & World Inc., New York.

CHURCH, JOSEPH (1961) *Language and the discovery of reality*, Random House, New York.

COHEN, STANLEY (ed.) (1971) *Images of deviance*, Penguin, Harmondsworth.

COLLINGWOOD, R. G. (1961) *The idea of history*, Oxford University Press, London.

COURTENAY, B. DE (1929) 'Einfluss der Sprache auf Weltanschauung und Stimmung', *Prace Filologiczne*, 14, Warsaw.

DAWE, ALAN (1970) 'The two sociologies', *British Journal of Sociology*, 21.

DESCARTES, R. (1965) *A discourse on method* (1637); *Meditations on the first philosophy* (1641); and *Principles of philosophy* (1642), J. M. Dent & Sons Ltd, London.

DILTHEY, W. (1931) *Gesammelte Schriften*, Bd. VIII: *Weltanschauungslehre*, Teubner, Leipzig and Berlin.

DOUGLAS, J. (1967) *The social meanings of suicide*, Princeton University Press, N.J.

DOUGLAS, J. (ed.) (1971) *Understanding everyday life: toward the reconstruction of sociological knowledge*, Routledge & Kegan Paul, London.

140

DOUGLAS, MARY (1971) 'In the nature of things', *New Society*, 9 December.
DUFRENNE, M. (1963) *Language and philosophy*, Indiana University Press, Bloomington.
DUFRENNE, M. (1967) *Phénoménologie de l'expérience esthétique*, Presses Universitaires de France, Paris.
DURKHEIM, E. (1915) *Elementary forms of religious life*, Allen & Unwin, London.
DURKHEIM, E. (1938) *Rules of sociological method*, Free Press, Chicago.
DURKHEIM, E. (1947) *The division of labour in society*, Free Press, Chicago.
DURKHEIM, E. (1951) *Suicide: a study in sociology*, Free Press, Chicago.
DURKHEIM, E. and MAUSS, M. (1963) *Primitive classification*, Cohen & West, London.
ESCARPIT, R. (1968) *Sociologie de la littérature*, Presses Universitaires de France, Paris.
FARIS, JAMES C. (1972) *Nuba personal art*, Duckworth, London.
FEARING, F. (1954) 'Examination of the conceptions of Benjamin Whorf in the light of theories of perception and cognition', in HOIJER, H. (ed.), *Language in culture (q.v.)*.
FILMER, P., PHILLIPSON, M., SILVERMAN, D. and WALSH, D. (1972) *New directions in sociological theory*, Collier-Macmillan, London.
FISCHER, E. (1964) *The necessity of art*, Penguin, Harmondsworth.
FRANCASTEL, PIERRE (1951) *Peinture et société: naissance et destruction d'un espace plastique de la renaissance au cubisme*, Audin, Lyon.
GADAMER, H.-G. (1965) *Wahrheit und Methode*, J. C. B. Mohr (Paul Siebeck), Tübingen.
GADAMER, H.-G. (1971) 'Rhetorik, Hermeneutik und Ideologiekritik. Metakritische Erörterungen zu *Wahrheit und Methode*', in APEL, K.-O. *et al., Hermeneutik und Ideologiekritik (q.v.)*.
GARDINER, PATRICK (1961) *The nature of historical explanation*, Oxford University Press, London.
GOLDMANN, L. (1964) *The hidden god*, Routledge & Kegan Paul, London.
GOLDMANN, L. (1967a) 'Sociology of literature—status and problems of method', *International Social Science Journal*, XIX, 4.
GOLDMANN, L. (1967b) 'Ideology and writing', Crosscurrents, *Times Literary Supplement*, 28 September.
GOLDMANN, L. (1969a) *The human sciences and philosophy*, Cape, London.
GOLDMANN, L. (1969b) *Pour une sociologie du roman*, Gallimard, Paris.
GOMBRICH, E. H. (1960) *Art and illusion: a study in the psychology of pictorial representation*, Phaidon Press, London.
GOMBRICH, E. H. (1969) *In search of cultural history*, Oxford University Press, London.
GOULDNER, A. (1971) *The coming crisis of Western sociology*, Heinemann, London.
GRAMONT, SANCHE DE (1970) 'There are no superior societies', in HAYES and HAYES (eds), *Claude Lévi-Strauss: the anthropologist as hero (q.v.)*.
GREENBERG, J. H. (1954) 'Concerning inferences from linguistic to non-linguistic data', in HOIJER, H. (ed.), *Language in culture (q.v.)*.
GURVITCH, G. (1971) *The social frameworks of knowledge*, Blackwell, Oxford.

141

BIBLIOGRAPHY

HABERMAS, J. (1966) 'Knowledge and interest', *Inquiry*, 9.
HABERMAS, J. (1970) *Zur Logik der Sozialwissenschaften*, Suhrkamp Verlag, Frankfurt am Main.
HABERMAS, J. (1971a) 'Zu Gadamers *Wahrheit und Methode*', in APEL, K.-O. et al., *Hermeneutik und Ideologiekritik (q.v.)*.
HABERMAS, J. (1971b) 'Der Universalitätsanspruch der Hermeneutik', in APEL, K.-O. et al., *Hermeneutik und Ideologiekritik (q.v.)*.
HABERMAS, J. (1972) *Knowledge and human interests*, Heinemann, London.
HAUSER, A. (1951) *The social history of art*, Routledge & Kegan Paul, London.
HAYES, E. N. and HAYES, T. (eds) (1970) *Claude Lévi-Strauss: the anthropologist as hero*, M.I.T., Cambridge, Massachusetts.
HEIDEGGER, M. (1962) *Being and time*, S.C.M. Press, London.
HENLE, PAUL (1965) *Language, thought and culture*, University of Michigan Press, Ann Arbor.
HERSKOVITS, M. (1951) 'Cultural and psychological reality', in ROHRER, J. H. and SHERIF, M. (eds), *Social psychology at the crossroads*, Harper, New York.
HERTZLER, J. O. (1965) *A sociology of language*, Random House, London.
HOCKETT, C. F. (1954) 'Chinese versus English: an exploration of the Whorfian hypothesis', in HOIJER, H. (ed.), *Language in culture (q.v.)*.
HOGG, JAMES (ed.) (1969) *Psychology and the visual arts*, Penguin, Harmondsworth.
HOIJER, H. (1951) 'Cultural implications of some Navaho linguistic categories', *Language*, 27.
HOIJER, H. (1953) 'The relation of language to culture', in KROEBER, A. L. et al., *Anthropology today*, University of Chicago Press.
HOIJER, H. (1954) 'The Sapir–Whorf hypothesis', in HOIJER (ed.), *Language in culture (q.v.)*.
HOIJER, H. (ed.) (1954) *Language in culture*, University of Chicago Press; American Anthropological Association Memoir, 79.
HUMBOLDT, W. VON (1960) *Über die Verschiedenheit der menschlichen Sprachbaues und Ihren Einfluss auf die geistige Entwickelung des Menschengeschlechts*, Dümmlers Verlag, Bonn.
HUSSERL, E. (1931) *Ideas*, Allen & Unwin, London.
HUSSERL, E. (1960) *Cartesian meditations*, Nijhoff, The Hague.
HUSSERL, E. (1965) *Phenomenology and the crisis of philosophy*, Harper & Row, New York.
HUSSERL, E. (1970) *The crisis of the European sciences and transcendental phenomenology* (trans. D. Carr), Northwestern University Press, Evanston, Ill.
HYMES, D. (ed.) (1964) *Language in culture and society: a reader in linguistics and anthropology*, Harper & Row, New York.
INGARDEN, ROMAN (1960) *Das literarische Kunstwerk*, Niemeyer, Tübingen.
INGARDEN, ROMAN (1961) 'Aesthetic experience and aesthetic object', *Philosophy and Phenomenological Research*, 21.
KAVOLIS, V. (1965) 'Artistic preferences of urban social classes', *Pacific Sociological Review*, Spring.
LANE, MICHAEL (ed.) (1970) *Structuralism: a reader* (Introduction), Cape, London.

LANGER, S. (1951) *Philosophy in a new key*, Mentor, New York.

LANGER, S. (1962) *Philosophical sketches*, Johns Hopkins Press, Baltimore, Maryland.

LAURENSON, D. (1969) 'A sociological study of authorship', *British Journal of Sociology*, XX, 3.

LEACH, E. (1967) 'Aesthetics', in *The institutions of primitive society* (A series of broadcast talks), Blackwell, Oxford.

LEACH, E. (ed.) (1968) *The structural study of myth and totemism*, Tavistock, London.

LEE, D. (1959) *Freedom and culture*, Prentice-Hall, Englewood Cliffs, N. J.

LEENHARDT, J. (1967) 'The sociology of literature—some stages in its history', *International Social Science Journal*, XIX, 4.

LENNEBERG, E. H. (1953) 'Cognition and ethnolinguistics', *Language*, 29.

LENNEBERG, E. H. and ROBERTS, J. M. (1956) 'The language of experience', *IUPAL*; Memoirs of I.J.A.L., No. 13, Bloomington.

LÉVI-STRAUSS, C. (1963) 'Réponses à quelques questions', *Esprit*, 11 November.

LÉVI-STRAUSS, C. (1964) 'Ouverture', *Le cru et le cuit—mythologiques*, Plon, Paris.

LÉVI-STRAUSS, C. (1967a) *Structural anthropology*, Anchor Books, New York.

LÉVI-STRAUSS, C. (1967b) *The scope of anthropology*, Cape, London.

LÉVI-STRAUSS, C. (1968a) *The savage mind*, Weidenfeld & Nicolson, London.

LÉVI-STRAUSS, C. (1968b) 'The story of Asdiwal', in LEACH, E. (ed.), *The structural study of myth and totemism*, (q.v).

LOWENTHAL, L. (1966) *Literature and the image of man. Studies of the European drama and novel, 1600–1900*, The Beacon Press, Boston.

LOWENTHAL, L. (1967) 'Literature and sociology', in THORPE, JAMES (ed.), *Relations of literary study*, Modern Language Association of America, New York.

MCHUGH, P. (1971) 'On the failure of positivism', in DOUGLAS, J. (ed.), *Understanding everyday life (q.v.)*.

MACKIE, ELIZABETH (1970) 'The sociology of the literary work: a critical study of the contribution of Goldmann and Benjamin to the methodology of the sociology of literature', M.Soc.Sc. dissertation, University of Birmingham.

MANNHEIM, K. (1958) 'The problem of generations', in *Essays on the sociology of knowledge*, Routledge & Kegan Paul, London.

MANNHEIM, K. (1966) 'Ideology and utopia', in *Ideology and utopia*, Routledge & Kegan Paul, London.

MANNHEIM, K. (1968) 'On the interpretation of "Weltanschauung"', in *Essays on the sociology of knowledge*, Routledge & Kegan Paul, London.

MARTIN, D. (1968) 'The sociology of knowledge and the nature of social knowledge', *British Journal of Sociology*, 19, 3.

MERLEAU-PONTY, M. (1951) 'Le philosophe et la sociologie', *Cahiers Internationaux de sociologie*, X; (also in *Signs*, Northwestern University Press, Evanston, Ill., 1964).

MERLEAU-PONTY, M. (1967) *The phenomenology of perception*, Routledge & Kegan Paul, London.

MERTON, R. (1957) *Social theory and social structure*, Free Press, Chicago.

MOORE, T. (undated) 'Claude Lévi-Strauss and the cultural sciences', Occasional Paper No. 4, Centre for Contemporary Cultural Studies, University of Birmingham.

NATANSON, M. (1962) *Literature, philosophy and the social sciences. Essays in existentialism and phenomenology*, Nijhoff, The Hague.

NATANSON, M. (1962) 'Toward a phenomenology of the aesthetic object', in *Literature, philosophy and the social sciences* (*q.v.*).

NATANSON, M. (1966) 'The phenomenology of Alfred Schutz', *Inquiry*, 9.

NATANSON, M. (1967) 'Introduction' to Schutz: *Collected Papers*, Vol. 1, *The problem of social reality*, Nijhoff, The Hague.

NEWMAN, S. (1954) 'Semantic problems in grammatical systems and lexemes: a search for method', in HOIJER, H. (ed.); *Language in culture* (*q.v.*).

PARSONS, T. (1949) *The structure of social action*, Free Press, Chicago.

PARSONS, T. (1951) *The social system*, Free Press, Chicago.

PARSONS, T. and SHILS, E. (eds) (1962) *Toward a general theory of action*, Harper & Row, New York.

PELLES, G. (1963) *Art, artists and society*, Prentice-Hall, Englewood Cliffs, N.J.

PIAGET, J. (1971) *Structuralism*, Routledge & Kegan Paul, London.

RADIN, PAUL (1960) 'The literature of primitive peoples', in STEIN, M. R. and VIDICH, A. J. (eds), *Identity and anxiety: survival of the person in mass society*, Free Press, New York.

READ, H. (1967) *Art and society*, Faber & Faber, London.

RICOEUR, P. (1963a) 'Structure et herméneutique', *Esprit*.

RICOEUR, P. (1963b) 'Réponses à quelques questions', *Esprit*.

RUNCIMAN, W. (1969) 'What is structuralism?', *British Journal of Sociology*, 20, 3.

SAPIR, E. (1949) *Language*, Harcourt Brace & World Inc., New York.

SAPIR, E. (1966) *Culture, language and personality*, University of California Press.

SARTRE, J.-P. (1957) *Being and nothingness: an essay on phenomenological ontology*, Methuen, London.

SCHELER, M. (1926) *Die Wissensformen und die Gesellschaft*, Leipzig.

SCHIWY, G. (1969) *Der französische Strukturalismus*, Rowohlt, Reinbek bei Hamburg.

SCHON, DONALD A. (1963) *Displacement of concepts*, Tavistock, London.

SCHUTZ, A. (1964) 'Making music together: a study in social relationship', in *Collected papers*, vol. 2, *Studies in social theory*, Nijhoff, The Hague.

SCHUTZ, A. (1964) 'Mozart and the philosophers', in *Collected papers*, vol. 2 (*q.v.*).

SCHUTZ, A. (1967) 'Common-sense and scientific interpretation', in *Collected papers*, vol. 1, *The problem of social reality*, Nijhoff, The Hague.

SCHUTZ, A. (1967) 'Concept and theory formation', in *Collected papers*, vol. 1 (*q.v.*).

SCHUTZ, A. (1967) 'Phenomenology and the social sciences', in *Collected papers*, vol. 1 (*q.v.*).

SCHUTZ, A. (1967) 'On multiple realities', in *Collected papers*, vol. 1 (*q.v.*).

SCHUTZ, A. (1967) 'Symbol, reality and society', in *Collected papers*, vol. 1 (*q.v.*).

SCHUTZ, A. (1972) *The phenomenology of the social world*, Heinemann, London.

SILBERMANN, A. (1968) 'A definition of the sociology of art', *International Social Science Journal*, XX, 4, *The arts in society*.

SMITH, M. W. (ed.) (1961) *The artist in tribal society: proceedings of a symposium held at the Royal Anthropological Institute*, Routledge & Kegan Paul, London.

SOMMERFELT, A. (1942) 'The social origin of linguistic categories', *Man*, 52.

SOROKIN, P. A. (1947) *Society, culture and personality: their structure and dynamics*, Harper, New York and London.

SPIEGELBERG, H. (1960a) *The phenomenological movement: a historical introduction* (2 vols), Nijhoff, The Hague.

SPIEGELBERG, H. (1960b) 'Husserl's phenomenology and existentialism', *Journal of Philosophy*, LXII.

STARK, W. (1967) *The sociology of knowledge. An essay in aid of a deeper understanding of the history of ideas*, Routledge & Kegan Paul, London.

STEINER, GEORGE (1970) 'Orpheus with his myths', in HAYES and HAYES (eds), *Claude Lévi-Strauss: the anthropologist as hero* (*q.v.*).

STRATHERN, ANDREW and STRATHERN, MARILYN (1971) *Self-decoration in Mount Hagen*, Duckworth, London.

THEVENAZ, PIERRE (1962) *What is phenomenology?*, Quadrangle Books, Chicago.

Times Literary Supplement (1967) Crosscurrents II, 28 September.

TIRYAKIAN, E. A. (1965) 'Existential phenomenology and the sociological tradition', *American Sociological Review*, 30.

VOSSLER, K. (1932) *The spirit of language in civilisation*, Kegan Paul, Trench, Trubner & Co. Ltd, London.

VYGOTSKY, L. (1967) *Thought and language*, M.I.T. Press, Cambridge, Massachusetts.

WATT, I. (1967) *The rise of the novel*, Chatto & Windus, London.

WEBB, R. K. (1955) *The British working-class reader, 1790–1848*, Allen & Unwin, London.

WEBER, M. (1930) *The Protestant ethic and the spirit of capitalism*, Allen & Unwin, London.

WEBER, M. (1947a) *Essays in sociology* (ed. H. H. Gerth and C. Wright Mills) Kegan Paul, Trench, Trubner & Co. Ltd, London (including 'Politics as a vocation' and 'Science as a vocation').

WEBER, M. (1947b) *The theory of social and economic organisation*, Hodge, London.

WEBER, M. (1968) *The methodology of the social sciences*, Free Press, New York.

WERKMEISTER, W. (1939) 'Natural languages as cultural indices', *Philosophy of Science*, 6.

WHORF, B. L. (1967) *Language, thought and reality*, M.I.T. Press, Cambridge, Massachusetts.

WINCH, P. (1971) *The idea of a social science and its relation to philosophy*, Routledge & Kegan Paul, London.

WINGERT, P. S. (1962) *Primitive art: its traditions and styles*, Oxford University Press, New York.

145

BIBLIOGRAPHY

WITTGENSTEIN, L. (1963) *Philosophical investigations*, Blackwell, Oxford.
WITTGENSTEIN, L. (1969) *On certainty*, Blackwell, Oxford.
WOLLHEIM, R. (1968) *Art and its objects*, Harper & Row, New York.
WOLFF, K. H. (ed.) (1960) *Emile Durkheim 1858–1917*, Ohio State University Press, Columbus.

Index

147

Routledge Social Science Series

Routledge & Kegan Paul   London, Henley and Boston

39 Store Street, London WC1E 7DD
Broadway House, Newtown Road,
Henley-on-Thames, Oxon RG9 1EN
9 Park Street, Boston, Mass. 02108

Contents

*Authors wishing to submit manuscripts for any series in
this catalogue should send them to the Social Science Editor,
Routledge & Kegan Paul Ltd, 39 Store Street,
London WC1E 7DD*

●*Books so marked are available in paperback
All books are in Metric Demy 8vo format (216 × 138mm approx.)*

International Library of Sociology

General Editor   John Rex

GENERAL SOCIOLOGY

Barnsley, J. H. The Social Reality of Ethics. *464 pp.*
Brown, Robert. Explanation in Social Science. *208 pp.*
● Rules and Laws in Sociology. *192 pp.*
Bruford, W. H. Chekhov and His Russia. *A Sociological Study. 244 pp.*
Burton, F. and **Carlen, P.** Official Discourse. *On Discourse Analysis, Government Publications, Ideology. About 140 pp.*
Cain, Maureen E. Society and the Policeman's Role. *326 pp.*
●**Fletcher, Colin.** Beneath the Surface. *An Account of Three Styles of Sociological Research. 221 pp.*
Gibson, Quentin. The Logic of Social Enquiry. *240 pp.*
Glucksmann, M. Structuralist Analysis in Contemporary Social Thought. *212 pp.*
Gurvitch, Georges. Sociology of Law. *Foreword by Roscoe Pound. 264 pp.*
Hinkle, R. Founding Theory of American Sociology 1883-1915. *About 350 pp.*
Homans, George C. Sentiments and Activities. *336 pp.*
Johnson, Harry M. Sociology: *a Systematic Introduction. Foreword by Robert K. Merton. 710 pp.*
●**Keat, Russell** and **Urry, John.** Social Theory as Science. *278 pp.*
Mannheim, Karl. Essays on Sociology and Social Psychology. *Edited by Paul Keckskemeti. With Editorial Note by Adolph Lowe. 344 pp.*
Martindale, Don. The Nature and Types of Sociological Theory. *292 pp.*
●**Maus, Heinz.** A Short History of Sociology. *234 pp.*
Myrdal, Gunnar. Value in Social Theory: *A Collection of Essays on Methodology. Edited by Paul Streeten. 332 pp.*
Ogburn, William F. and **Nimkoff, Meyer F.** A Handbook of Sociology. *Preface by Karl Mannheim. 656 pp. 46 figures. 35 tables.*
Parsons, Talcott, and **Smelser, Neil J.** Economy and Society: *A Study in the Integration of Economic and Social Theory. 362 pp.*
Podgórecki, Adam. Practical Social Sciences. *About 200 pp.*
Raffel, S. Matters of Fact. *A Sociological Inquiry. 152 pp.*
●**Rex, John.** (Ed.) Approaches to Sociology. *Contributions by Peter Abell,* Sociology and the Demystification of the Modern World. *282 pp.*
●**Rex, John** (Ed.) Approaches to Sociology. *Contributions by Peter Abell, Frank Bechhofer, Basil Bernstein, Ronald Fletcher, David Frisby, Miriam Glucksmann, Peter Lassman, Herminio Martins, John Rex, Roland Robertson, John Westergaard and Jock Young. 302 pp.*
Rigby, A. Alternative Realities. *352 pp.*
Roche, M. Phenomenology, Language and the Social Sciences. *374 pp.*
Sahay, A. Sociological Analysis. *220 pp.*

Strasser, Hermann. The Normative Structure of Sociology. *Conservative and Emancipatory Themes in Social Thought. About 340 pp.*
Strong, P. Ceremonial Order of the Clinic. *About 250 pp.*
Urry, John. Reference Groups and the Theory of Revolution. *244 pp.*
Weinberg, E. Development of Sociology in the Soviet Union. *173 pp.*

FOREIGN CLASSICS OF SOCIOLOGY

● **Gerth, H. H.** and **Mills, C. Wright.** From Max Weber: *Essays in Sociology. 502 pp.*
● **Tönnies, Ferdinand.** Community and Association. *(Gemeinschaft and Gesellschaft.) Translated and Supplemented by Charles P. Loomis. Foreword by Pitirim A. Sorokin. 334 pp.*

SOCIAL STRUCTURE

Andreski, Stanislav. Military Organization and Society. *Foreword by Professor A. R. Radcliffe-Brown. 226 pp. 1 folder.*
Carlton, Eric. Ideology and Social Order. *Foreword by Professor Philip Abrahams. About 320 pp.*
Coontz, Sydney H. Population Theories and the Economic Interpretation. *202 pp.*
Coser, Lewis. The Functions of Social Conflict. *204 pp.*
Dickie-Clark, H. F. Marginal Situation: *A Sociological Study of a Coloured Group. 240 pp. 11 tables.*
Giner, S. and **Archer, M. S.** (Eds.). Contemporary Europe. *Social Structures and Cultural Patterns. 336 pp.*
● **Glaser, Barney** and **Strauss, Anselm L.** Status Passage. *A Formal Theory. 212 pp.*
Glass, D. V. (Ed.) Social Mobility in Britain. *Contributions by J. Berent, T. Bottomore, R. C. Chambers, J. Floud, D. V. Glass, J. R. Hall, H. T. Himmelweit, R. K. Kelsall, F. M. Martin, C. A. Moser, R. Mukherjee, and W. Ziegel. 420 pp.*
Kelsall, R. K. Higher Civil Servants in Britain: *From 1870 to the Present Day. 268 pp. 31 tables.*
● **Lawton, Denis.** Social Class, Language and Education. *192 pp.*
McLeish, John. The Theory of Social Change: *Four Views Considered. 128 pp.*
● **Marsh, David C.** The Changing Social Structure of England and Wales, 1871-1961. *Revised edition. 288 pp.*
Menzies, Ken. Talcott Parsons and the Social Image of Man. *About 208 pp.*
● **Mouzelis, Nicos.** Organization and Bureaucracy. *An Analysis of Modern Theories. 240 pp.*
Ossowski, Stanislaw. Class Structure in the Social Consciousness. *210 pp.*
● **Podgórecki, Adam.** Law and Society. *302 pp.*
Renner, Karl. Institutions of Private Law and Their Social Functions. *Edited, with an Introduction and Notes, by O. Kahn-Freud. Translated by Agnes Schwarzschild. 316 pp.*

Rex, J. and **Tomlinson, S.** Colonial Immigrants in a British City. *A Class Analysis. 368 pp.*
Smooha, S. Israel: Pluralism and Conflict. *472 pp.*
Wesolowski, W. Class, Strata and Power. *Trans. and with Introduction by G. Kolankiewicz. 160 pp.*
Zureik, E. Palestinians in Israel. *A Study in Internal Colonialism. 264 pp.*

SOCIOLOGY AND POLITICS

Acton, T. A. Gypsy Politics and Social Change. *316 pp.*
Burton, F. Politics of Legitimacy. *Struggles in a Belfast Community. 250 pp.*
Etzioni-Halevy, E. Political Manipulation and Administrative Power. *A Comparative Study. About 200 pp.*
●**Hechter, Michael.** Internal Colonialism. *The Celtic Fringe in British National Development, 1536–1966. 380 pp.*
Kornhauser, William. The Politics of Mass Society. *272 pp. 20 tables.*
Korpi, W. The Working Class in Welfare Capitalism. *Work, Unions and Politics in Sweden. 472 pp.*
Kroes, R. Soldiers and Students. *A Study of Right- and Left-wing Students. 174 pp.*
Martin, Roderick. Sociology of Power. *About 272 pp.*
Myrdal, Gunnar. The Political Element in the Development of Economic Theory. *Translated from the German by Paul Streeten. 282 pp.*
Wong, S.-L. Sociology and Socialism in Contemporary China. *160 pp.*
Wootton, Graham. Workers, Unions and the State. *188 pp.*

CRIMINOLOGY

Ancel, Marc. Social Defence: *A Modern Approach to Criminal Problems. Foreword by Leon Radzinowicz. 240 pp.*
Athens, L. Violent Criminal Acts and Actors. *About 150 pp.*
Cain, Maureen E. Society and the Policeman's Role. *326 pp.*
Cloward, Richard A. and **Ohlin, Lloyd E.** Delinquency and Opportunity: *A Theory of Delinquent Gangs. 248 pp.*
Downes, David M. The Delinquent Solution. *A Study in Subcultural Theory. 296 pp.*
Friedlander, Kate. The Psycho-Analytical Approach to Juvenile Delinquency: *Theory, Case Studies, Treatment. 320 pp.*
Gleuck, Sheldon and **Eleanor.** Family Environment and Delinquency. *With the statistical assistance of Rose W. Kneznek. 340 pp.*
Lopez-Rey, Manuel. Crime. *An Analytical Appraisal. 288 pp.*
Mannheim, Hermann. Comparative Criminology: *a Text Book. Two volumes. 442 pp. and 380 pp.*
Morris, Terence. The Criminal Area: *A Study in Social Ecology. Foreword by Hermann Mannheim. 232 pp. 25 tables. 4 maps.*
Podgorecki, A. and **Łos, M.** *Multidimensional Sociology. About 380 pp.*
Rock, Paul. Making People Pay. *338 pp.*

● **Taylor, Ian, Walton, Paul,** and **Young, Jock.** The New Criminology. *For a Social Theory of Deviance. 325 pp.*
● **Taylor, Ian, Walton, Paul** and **Young, Jock.** (Eds) Critical Criminology. *268 pp.*

SOCIAL PSYCHOLOGY

Bagley, Christopher. The Social Psychology of the Epileptic Child. *320 pp.*
Brittan, Arthur. Meanings and Situations. *224 pp.*
Carroll, J. Break-Out from the Crystal Palace. *200 pp.*
● **Fleming, C. M.** Adolescence: Its Social Psychology. *With an Introduction to recent findings from the fields of Anthropology, Physiology, Medicine, Psychometrics and Sociometry. 288 pp.*
● The Social Psychology of Education: *An Introduction and Guide to Its Study. 136 pp.*
Linton, Ralph. The Cultural Background of Personality. *132 pp.*
● **Mayo, Elton.** The Social Problems of an Industrial Civilization. *With an Appendix on the Political Problem. 180 pp.*
Ottaway, A. K. C. Learning Through Group Experience. *176 pp.*
Plummer, Ken. Sexual Stigma. *An Interactionist Account. 254 pp.*
● **Rose, Arnold M.** (Ed.) Human Behaviour and Social Processes: *an Interactionist Approach. Contributions by Arnold M. Rose, Ralph H. Turner, Anselm Strauss, Everett C. Hughes, E. Franklin Frazier, Howard S. Becker et al. 696 pp.*
Smelser, Neil J. Theory of Collective Behaviour. *448 pp.*
Stephenson, Geoffrey M. The Development of Conscience. *128 pp.*
Young, Kimball. Handbook of Social Psychology. *658 pp. 16 figures. 10 tables.*

SOCIOLOGY OF THE FAMILY

Bell, Colin R. Middle Class Families: *Social and Geographical Mobility. 224 pp.*
Burton, Lindy. Vulnerable Children. *272 pp.*
Gavron, Hannah. The Captive Wife: *Conflicts of Household Mothers. 190 pp.*
George, Victor and **Wilding, Paul.** Motherless Families. *248 pp.*
Klein, Josephine. Samples from English Cultures.
   1. Three Preliminary Studies and Aspects of Adult Life in England. *447 pp.*
   2. Child-Rearing Practices and Index. *247 pp.*
Klein, Viola. The Feminine Character. *History of an Ideology. 244 pp.*
McWhinnie, Alexina M. Adopted Children. *How They Grow Up. 304 pp.*
● **Morgan, D. H. J.** Social Theory and the Family. *About 320 pp.*
● **Myrdal, Alva** and **Klein, Viola.** Women's Two Roles: *Home and Work. 238 pp. 27 tables.*

Parsons, Talcott and **Bales, Robert F.** Family: Socialization and Inter-action Process. *In collaboration with James Olds, Morris Zelditch and Philip E. Slater. 456 pp. 50 figures and tables.*

SOCIAL SERVICES

Bastide, Roger. The Sociology of Mental Disorder. *Translated from the French by Jean McNeil. 260 pp.*

Carlebach, Julius. Caring For Children in Trouble. *266 pp.*

George, Victor. Foster Care. *Theory and Practice. 234 pp.*
Social Security: *Beveridge and After. 258 pp.*

George, V. and **Wilding, P.** Motherless Families. *248 pp.*

● **Goetschius, George W.** Working with Community Groups. *256 pp.*

Goetschius, George W. and **Tash, Joan.** Working with Unattached Youth. *416 pp.*

Heywood, Jean S. Children in Care. *The Development of the Service for the Deprived Child. Third revised edition. 284 pp.*

King, Roy D., Ranes, Norma V. and **Tizard, Jack.** Patterns of Residential Care. *356 pp.*

Leigh, John. Young People and Leisure. *256 pp.*

● **Mays, John.** (Ed.) Penelope Hall's Social Services of England and Wales. *About 324 pp.*

Morris, Mary. Voluntary Work and the Welfare State. *300 pp.*

Nokes, P. L. The Professional Task in Welfare Practice. *152 pp.*

Timms, Noel. Psychiatric Social Work in Great Britain (1939-1962). *280 pp.*

● Social Casework: *Principles and Practice. 256 pp.*

SOCIOLOGY OF EDUCATION

Banks, Olive. Parity and Prestige in English Secondary Education: a Study in Educational Sociology. *272 pp.*

● **Blyth, W. A. L.** English Primary Education. *A Sociological Description.* 2. Background. *168 pp.*

Collier, K. G. The Social Purposes of Education: *Personal and Social Values in Education. 268 pp.*

Evans, K. M. Sociometry and Education. *158 pp.*

● **Ford, Julienne.** Social Class and the Comprehensive School. *192 pp.*

Foster, P. J. Education and Social Change in Ghana. *336 pp. 3 maps.*

Fraser, W. R. Education and Society in Modern France. *150 pp.*

Grace, Gerald R. Role Conflict and the Teacher. *150 pp.*

Hans, Nicholas. New Trends in Education in the Eighteenth Century. *278 pp. 19 tables.*

● Comparative Education: *A Study of Educational Factors and Traditions. 360 pp.*

● **Hargreaves, David.** Interpersonal Relations and Education. *432 pp.*

● Social Relations in a Secondary School. *240 pp.*

School Organization and Pupil Involvement. *A Study of Secondary Schools.*

● **Mannheim, Karl** and **Stewart, W.A.C.** An Introduction to the Sociology of Education. *206 pp.*

● **Musgrove, F.** Youth and the Social Order. *176 pp.*

● **Ottaway, A. K. C.** Education and Society: An Introduction to the Sociology of Education. *With an Introduction by W. O. Lester Smith. 212 pp.*

Peers, Robert. Adult Education: *A Comparative Study. Revised edition. 398 pp.*

Stratta, Erica. The Education of Borstal Boys. *A Study of their Educational Experiences prior to, and during, Borstal Training. 256 pp.*

● **Taylor, P. H., Reid, W. A.** and **Holley, B. J.** The English Sixth Form. *A Case Study in Curriculum Research. 198 pp.*

SOCIOLOGY OF CULTURE

Eppel, E. M. and **M.** Adolescents and Morality: *A Study of some Moral Values and Dilemmas of Working Adolescents in the Context of a changing Climate of Opinion. Foreword by W. J. H. Sprott. 268 pp. 39 tables.*

● **Fromm, Erich.** The Fear of Freedom. *286 pp.*

● The Sane Society. *400 pp.*

Johnson, L. The Cultural Critics. *From Matthew Arnold to Raymond Williams. 233 pp.*

Mannheim, Karl. Essays on the Sociology of Culture. *Edited by Ernst Mannheim in co-operation with Paul Kecskemeti. Editorial Note by Adolph Lowe. 280 pp.*

Zijderfeld, A. C. On Clichés. *The Supersedure of Meaning by Function in Modernity. About 132 pp.*

SOCIOLOGY OF RELIGION

Argyle, Michael and **Beit-Hallahmi, Benjamin.** The Social Psychology of Religion. *About 256 pp.*

Glasner, Peter E. The Sociology of Secularisation. *A Critique of a Concept. About 180 pp.*

Hall, J. R. The Ways Out. *Utopian Communal Groups in an Age of Babylon. 280 pp.*

Ranson, S., Hinings, B. and **Bryman, A.** Clergy, Ministers and Priests. *216 pp.*

Stark, Werner. The Sociology of Religion. *A Study of Christendom.*
Volume II. *Sectarian Religion. 368 pp.*
Volume III. *The Universal Church. 464 pp.*
Volume IV. *Types of Religious Man. 352 pp.*
Volume V. *Types of Religious Culture. 464 pp.*

Turner, B. S. Weber and Islam. *216 pp.*

Watt, W. Montgomery. Islam and the Integration of Society. *320 pp.*

SOCIOLOGY OF ART AND LITERATURE
Jarvie, Ian C. Towards a Sociology of the Cinema. *A Comparative Essay on the Structure and Functioning of a Major Entertainment Industry.* *405 pp.*
Rust, Frances S. Dance in Society. *An Analysis of the Relationships between the Social Dance and Society in England from the Middle Ages to the Present Day. 256 pp. 8 pp. of plates.*
Schücking, L. L. The Sociology of Literary Taste. *112 pp.*
Wolff, Janet. Hermeneutic Philosophy and the Sociology of Art. *150 pp.*

SOCIOLOGY OF KNOWLEDGE
Diesing, P. Patterns of Discovery in the Social Sciences. *262 pp.*
● **Douglas, J. D.** (Ed.) Understanding Everyday Life. *370 pp.*
Glasner, B. Essential Interactionism. *About 220 pp.*
● **Hamilton, P.** Knowledge and Social Structure. *174 pp.*
Jarvie, I. C. Concepts and Society. *232 pp.*
Mannheim, Karl. Essays on the Sociology of Knowledge. *Edited by Paul Kecskemeti. Editorial Note by Adolph Lowe. 353 pp.*
Remmling, Gunter W. The Sociology of Karl Mannheim. *With a Bibliographical Guide to the Sociology of Knowledge, Ideological Analysis, and Social Planning. 255 pp.*
Remmling, Gunter W. (Ed.) Towards the Sociology of Knowledge. *Origin and Development of a Sociological Thought Style. 463 pp.*

URBAN SOCIOLOGY
Aldridge, M. The British New Towns. *A Programme Without a Policy. About 250 pp.*
Ashworth, William. The Genesis of Modern British Town Planning: *A Study in Economic and Social History of the Nineteenth and Twentieth Centuries. 288 pp.*
Brittan, A. The Privatised World. *196 pp.*
Cullingworth, J. B. Housing Needs and Planning Policy: *A Restatement of the Problems of Housing Need and 'Overspill' in England and Wales. 232 pp. 44 tables. 8 maps.*
Dickinson, Robert E. City and Region: *A Geographical Interpretation. 608 pp. 125 figures.*
The West European City: *A Geographical Interpretation. 600 pp. 129 maps. 29 plates.*
Humphreys, Alexander J. New Dubliners: *Urbanization and the Irish Family. Foreword by George C. Homans. 304 pp.*
Jackson, Brian. Working Class Community: *Some General Notions raised by a Series of Studies in Northern England. 192 pp.*
● **Mann, P. H.** An Approach to Urban Sociology. *240 pp.*
Mellor, J. R. Urban Sociology in an Urbanized Society. *326 pp.*
Morris, R. N. and **Mogey, J.** The Sociology of Housing. *Studies at Berinsfield. 232 pp. 4 pp. plates.*

Rosser, C. and **Harris, C.** The Family and Social Change. *A Study of Family and Kinship in a South Wales Town. 352 pp. 8 maps.*

● **Stacey, Margaret, Batsone, Eric, Bell, Colin** and **Thurcott, Anne.** Power, Persistence and Change. *A Second Study of Banbury. 196 pp.*

RURAL SOCIOLOGY

Mayer, Adrian C. Peasants in the Pacific. *A Study of Fiji Indian Rural Society. 248 pp. 20 plates.*

Williams, W. M. The Sociology of an English Village: *Gosforth. 272 pp. 12 figures. 13 tables.*

SOCIOLOGY OF INDUSTRY AND DISTRIBUTION

Dunkerley, David. The Foreman. *Aspects of Task and Structure. 192 pp.*

Eldridge, J. E. T. Industrial Disputes. *Essays in the Sociology of Industrial Relations. 288 pp.*

Hollowell, Peter G. The Lorry Driver. *272 pp.*

● **Oxaal, I., Barnett, T.** and **Booth, D.** (Eds) Beyond the Sociology of Development. *Economy and Society in Latin America and Africa. 295 pp.*

Smelser, Neil J. Social Change in the Industrial Revolution: *An Application of Theory to the Lancashire Cotton Industry, 1770–1840. 468 pp. 12 figures. 14 tables.*

Watson, T. J. The Personnel Managers. *A Study in the Sociology of Work and Employment. 262 pp.*

ANTHROPOLOGY

Brandel-Syrier, Mia. Reeftown Elite. *A Study of Social Mobility in a Modern African Community on the Reef. 376 pp.*

Dickie-Clark, H. F. The Marginal Situation. *A Sociological Study of a Coloured Group. 236 pp.*

Dube, S. C. Indian Village. *Foreword by Morris Edward Opler. 276 pp. 4 plates.*

India's Changing Villages: *Human Factors in Community Development. 260 pp. 8 plates. 1 map.*

Firth, Raymond. Malay Fishermen. *Their Peasant Economy. 420 pp. 17 pp. plates.*

Gulliver, P. H. Social Control in an African Society: a Study of the Arusha, Agricultural Masai of Northern Tanganyika. *320 pp. 8 plates. 10 figures.*

Family Herds. *288 pp.*

Jarvie, Ian C. The Revolution in Anthropology. *268 pp.*

Little, Kenneth L. Mende of Sierra Leone. *308 pp. and folder.*

Negroes in Britain. *With a New Introduction and Contemporary Study by Leonard Bloom. 320 pp.*

Madan, G. R. Western Sociologists on Indian Society. *Marx, Spencer, Weber, Durkheim, Pareto. 384 pp.*

Mayer, A. C. Peasants in the Pacific. *A Study of Fiji Indian Rural Society. 248 pp.*

Meer, Fatima. Race and Suicide in South Africa. *325 pp.*

Smith, Raymond T. The Negro Family in British Guiana: *Family Structure and Social Status in the Villages. With a Foreword by Meyer Fortes. 314 pp. 8 plates. 1 figure. 4 maps.*

SOCIOLOGY AND PHILOSOPHY

Barnsley, John H. The Social Reality of Ethics. *A Comparative Analysis of Moral Codes. 448 pp.*

Diesing, Paul. Patterns of Discovery in the Social Sciences. *362 pp.*

● **Douglas, Jack D.** (Ed.) Understanding Everyday Life. *Toward the Reconstruction of Sociological Knowledge. Contributions by Alan F. Blum, Aaron W. Cicourel, Norman K. Denzin, Jack D. Douglas, John Heeren, Peter McHugh, Peter K. Manning, Melvin Power, Matthew Speier, Roy Turner, D. Lawrence Wieder, Thomas P. Wilson and Don H. Zimmerman. 370 pp.*

Gorman, Robert A. The Dual Vision. *Alfred Schutz and the Myth of Phenomenological Social Science. About 300 pp.*

Jarvie, Ian C. Concepts and Society. *216 pp.*

Kilminster, R. Praxis and Method. *A Sociological Dialogue with Lukács, Gramsci and the early Frankfurt School. About 304 pp.*

● **Pelz, Werner.** The Scope of Understanding in Sociology. *Towards a More Radical Reorientation in the Social Humanistic Sciences. 283 pp.*

Roche, Maurice. Phenomenology, Language and the Social Sciences. *371 pp.*

Sahay, Arun. Sociological Analysis. *212 pp.*

Slater, P. Origin and Significance of the Frankfurt School. *A Marxist Perspective. About 192 pp.*

Spurling, L. Phenomenology and the Social World. *The Philosophy of Merleau-Ponty and its Relation to the Social Sciences. 222 pp.*

Wilson, H. T. The American Ideology. *Science, Technology and Organization as Modes of Rationality. 368 pp.*

International Library of Anthropology

General Editor   Adam Kuper

Ahmed, A. S. Millenium and Charisma Among Pathans. *A Critical Essay in Social Anthropology. 192 pp.*
Pukhtun Economy and Society. *About 360 pp.*

Brown, Paula. The Chimbu. *A Study of Change in the New Guinea Highlands. 151 pp.*

Foner, N. Jamaica Farewell. *200 pp.*

Gudeman, Stephen. Relationships, Residence and the Individual. *A Rural Panamanian Community. 288 pp. 11 plates, 5 figures, 2 maps, 10 tables.*

  The Demise of a Rural Economy. *From Subsistence to Capitalism in a Latin American Village. 160 pp.*

Hamnett, Ian. Chieftainship and Legitimacy. *An Anthropological Study of Executive Law in Lesotho. 163 pp.*

Hanson, F. Allan. Meaning in Culture. *127 pp.*

Humphreys, S. C. Anthropology and the Greeks. *288 pp.*

Karp, I. Fields of Change Among the Iteso of Kenya. *140 pp.*

Lloyd, P. C. Power and Independence. *Urban Africans' Perception of Social Inequality. 264 pp.*

Parry, J. P. Caste and Kinship in Kangra. *352 pp. Illustrated.*

Pettigrew, Joyce. Robber Noblemen. *A Study of the Political System of the Sikh Jats. 284 pp.*

Street, Brian V. The Savage in Literature. *Representations of 'Primitive' Society in English Fiction, 1858–1920. 207 pp.*

Van Den Berghe, Pierre L. Power and Privilege at an African University. *278 pp.*

International Library of Social Policy

General Editor   Kathleen Jones

Bayley, M. Mental Handicap and Community Care. *426 pp.*

Bottoms, A. E. and **McClean, J. D.** Defendants in the Criminal Process. *284 pp.*

Butler, J. R. Family Doctors and Public Policy. *208 pp.*

Davies, Martin. Prisoners of Society. *Attitudes and Aftercare. 204 pp.*

Gittus, Elizabeth. Flats, Families and the Under-Fives. *285 pp.*

Holman, Robert. Trading in Children. *A Study of Private Fostering. 355 pp.*

Jeffs, A. Young People and the Youth Service. *About 180 pp.*

Jones, Howard, and **Cornes, Paul.** Open Prisons. *288 pp.*

Jones, Kathleen. History of the Mental Health Service. *428 pp.*

Jones, Kathleen, with **Brown, John, Cunningham, W. J., Roberts, Julian** and **Williams, Peter.** Opening the Door. *A Study of New Policies for the Mentally Handicapped. 278 pp.*

Karn, Valerie. Retiring to the Seaside. *About 280 pp. 2 maps. Numerous tables.*

King, R. D. and **Elliot, K. W.** Albany: Birth of a Prison—End of an Era. *394 pp.*

Thomas, J. E. The English Prison Officer since 1850: *A Study in Conflict. 258 pp.*

Walton, R. G. Women in Social Work. *303 pp.*

● **Woodward, J.** To Do the Sick No Harm. *A Study of the British Voluntary Hospital System to 1875. 234 pp.*

International Library of Welfare and Philosophy

General Editors Noel Timms and David Watson

● **McDermott, F. E.** (Ed.) Self-Determination in Social Work. *A Collection of Essays on Self-determination and Related Concepts by Philosophers and Social Work Theorists. Contributors: F. B. Biestek, S. Bernstein, A. Keith-Lucas, D. Sayer, H. H. Perelman, C. Whittington, R. F. Stalley, F. E. McDermott, I. Berlin, H. J. McCloskey, H. L. A. Hart, J. Wilson, A. I. Melden, S. I. Benn. 254 pp.*

● **Plant, Raymond.** Community and Ideology. *104 pp.*

Ragg, Nicholas M. People Not Cases. *A Philosophical Approach to Social Work. About 250 pp.*

● **Timms, Noel** and **Watson, David.** (Eds) Talking About Welfare. *Readings in Philosophy and Social Policy. Contributors: T. H. Marshall, R. B. Brandt, G. H. von Wright, K. Nielsen, M. Cranston, R. M. Titmuss, R. S. Downie, E. Telfer, D. Donnison, J. Benson, P. Leonard, A. Keith-Lucas, D. Walsh, I. T. Ramsey. 320 pp.*

● (Eds). Philosophy in Social Work. *250 pp.*

● **Weale, A.** Equality and Social Policy. *164 pp.*

Primary Socialization, Language and Education

General Editor Basil Bernstein

Adlam, Diana S., *with the assistance of Geoffrey Turner and Lesley Lineker.* Code in Context. *About 272 pp.*

Bernstein, Basil. Class, Codes and Control. *3 volumes.*

● 1. *Theoretical Studies Towards a Sociology of Language. 254 pp.*

2. *Applied Studies Towards a Sociology of Language. 377 pp.*

● 3. *Towards a Theory of Educational Transmission. 167 pp.*

Brandis, W. and **Bernstein, B.** Selection and Control. *176 pp.*

Brandis, Walter and **Henderson, Dorothy.** Social Class, Language and Communication. *288 pp.*

Cook-Gumperz, Jenny. Social Control and Socialization. *A Study of Class Differences in the Language of Maternal Control. 290 pp.*

● **Gahagan, D. M** and **G. A.** Talk Reform. *Exploration in Language for Infant School Children. 160 pp.*

Hawkins, P. R. Social Class, the Nominal Group and Verbal Strategies. *About 220 pp.*

Robinson, W. P. and **Rackstraw, Susan D. A.** A Question of Answers. *2 volumes. 192 pp. and 180 pp.*

Turner, Geoffrey J. and **Mohan, Bernard A.** A Linguistic Description and Computer Programme for Children's Speech. *208 pp.*

Reports of the Institute of Community Studies

Baker, J. The Neighbourhood Advice Centre. A Community Project in Camden. *320 pp.*

● **Cartwright, Ann.** Patients and their Doctors. *A Study of General Practice. 304 pp.*

Dench, Geoff. Maltese in London. *A Case-study in the Erosion of Ethnic Consciousness. 302 pp.*

Jackson, Brian and **Marsden, Dennis.** Education and the Working Class: *Some General Themes raised by a Study of 88 Working-class Children in a Northern Industrial City. 268 pp. 2 folders.*

Marris, Peter. The Experience of Higher Education. *232 pp. 27 tables.*

● Loss and Change. *192 pp.*

Marris, Peter and **Rein, Martin.** Dilemmas of Social Reform. *Poverty and Community Action in the United States. 256 pp.*

Marris, Peter and **Somerset, Anthony.** African Businessmen. *A Study of Entrepreneurship and Development in Keyna. 256 pp.*

Mills, Richard. Young Outsiders: *a Study in Alternative Communities. 216 pp.*

Runciman, W. G. Relative Deprivation and Social Justice. *A Study of Attitudes to Social Inequality in Twentieth-Century England. 352 pp.*

Willmott, Peter. Adolescent Boys in East London. *230 pp.*

Willmott, Peter and **Young, Michael.** Family and Class in a London Suburb. *202 pp. 47 tables.*

Young, Michael and **McGeeney, Patrick.** Learning Begins at Home. *A Study of a Junior School and its Parents. 128 pp.*

Young, Michael and **Willmott, Peter.** Family and Kinship in East London. *Foreword by Richard M. Titmuss. 252 pp. 39 tables.*

The Symmetrical Family. *410 pp.*

Reports of the Institute for Social Studies in Medical Care

Cartwright, Ann, Hockey, Lisbeth and **Anderson, John J.** Life Before Death. *310 pp.*

Dunnell, Karen and **Cartwright, Ann.** Medicine Takers, Prescribers and Hoarders. *190 pp.*

Farrell, C. My Mother Said. . . . *A Study of the Way Young People Learned About Sex and Birth Control. 200 pp.*

Medicine, Illness and Society

General Editor W. M. Williams

Hall, David J. Social Relations & Innovation. *Changing the State of Play in Hospitals. 232 pp.*

Hall, David J., and **Stacey, M.** (Eds) Beyond Separation. *234 pp.*

Robinson, David. The Process of Becoming Ill. *142 pp.*

Stacey, Margaret *et al.* Hospitals, Children and Their Families. *The Report of a Pilot Study. 202 pp.*

Stimson G. V. and **Webb, B.** Going to See the Doctor. *The Consultation Process in General Practice. 155 pp.*

Monographs in Social Theory

General Editor Arthur Brittan

● **Barnes, B.** Scientific Knowledge and Sociological Theory. *192 pp.*

Bauman, Zygmunt. Culture as Praxis. *204 pp.*

● **Dixon, Keith.** Sociological Theory. *Pretence and Possibility. 142 pp.*

Meltzer, B. N., Petras, J. W. and **Reynolds, L. T.** Symbolic Interactionism. *Genesis, Varieties and Criticisms. 144 pp.*

● **Smith, Anthony D.** The Concept of Social Change. *A Critique of the Functionalist Theory of Social Change. 208 pp.*

Routledge Social Science Journals

The British Journal of Sociology. *Editor – Angus Stewart; Associate Editor – Leslie Sklair. Vol. 1, No. 1 – March 1950 and Quarterly. Roy. 8vo. All back issues available. An international journal publishing original papers in the field of sociology and related areas.*

Community Work. *Edited by David Jones and Marjorie Mayo. 1973. Published annually.*

Economy and Society. *Vol. 1, No. 1. February 1972 and Quarterly. Metric Roy. 8vo. A journal for all social scientists covering sociology, philosophy, anthropology, economics and history. All back numbers available.*

Ethnic and Racial Studies. *Editor – John Stone. Vol. 1 – 1978. Published quarterly.*

Religion. Journal of Religion and Religions. *Chairman of Editorial Board, Ninian Smart. Vol. 1, No. 1, Spring 1971. A journal with an interdisciplinary approach to the study of the phenomena of religion. All back numbers available.*

Sociology of Health and Illness. *A Journal of Medical Sociology. Editor – Alan Davies; Associate Editor – Ray Jobling. Vol. 1, Spring 1979. Published 3 times per annum.*

Year Book of Social Policy in Britain, The. *Edited by Kathleen Jones. 1971. Published annually.*

Social and Psychological Aspects of Medical Practice

Editor Trevor Silverstone

Lader, Malcolm. Psychophysiology of Mental Illness. *280 pp.*

● **Silverstone, Trevor** and **Turner, Paul.** Drug Treatment in Psychiatry. *Revised edition. 256 pp.*

Whiteley, J. S. and **Gordon, J.** Group Approaches in Psychiatry. *256 pp.*

Printed in Great Britain by
Lowe & Brydone Printers Limited, Thetford, Norfolk